Mo...
For
Mother's Day
This
One of the loveliest
Books
Found for a long
Time
With love from
Guy and Rosemary

GRACE IN WINTER

GRACE IN WINTER

Rutherford in verse

Faith Cook

'I see grace groweth best in winter.'
Samuel Rutherford to Lady Culross

THE BANNER OF TRUTH

THE BANNER OF TRUTH TRUST
3 Murrayfield Road, Edinburgh EH12 6EL
P.O. Box 621, Carlisle, Pennsylvania 17013, U.S.A.

★

© *Faith Cook 1989*
First Published 1989
ISBN 0 85151 555 X

★

Typeset in 10½/12pt Linotron Plantin
at The Spartan Press Limited,
Lymington, Hants
Printed and bound in Great Britain by
The Camelot Press Ltd, Southampton

FOREWORD

What an experience it must have been, a few centuries ago, for one to wend one's way, Sabbath by Sabbath, to the kirk of Anwoth and there with other prayerful worshippers be with Samuel Rutherford and hear him tell of the boundless and unsearchable riches of the saving and sanctifying grace of God in the Lord Jesus Christ. Enriched indeed would one have been. Since that time there have been many who also have been blessedly enriched through learning about him – his person, life and, above all, his message concerning Christ 'who of God is made unto us wisdom and righteousness and sanctification and redemption.' For much of this we are indebted to those who have written about him and very much so to those who have brought out editions of his own works, such as his *Communion Sermons, Christ Dying and Drawing Sinners to Himself, Lex Rex, The Triumph of Faith* and the *Letters of Samuel Rutherford*.

One will readily appreciate on reading *Grace in Winter* that the author, Mrs Faith Cook, is of one heart and soul with Samuel Rutherford in her interpreting his prose into verse. She has accomplished something refreshingly and beautifully new. In this most acceptable book there is the unison of praising hearts and harps. The song of the redeemed is theirs, 'Worthy is the Lamb for He was slain for us.' In our day when many are deluded by the false joys of prosperity and pleasures, *Grace in Winter* bids us in word and song to 'Believe, rejoice, sing and triumph'.

JOCK PURVES
Deans, Livingston, West Lothian

AN EXPLANATION . . .

'The sands of time are sinking,
The dawn of heaven breaks . . .'

These are the opening lines of the well-loved hymn by Anne Ross Cousin that is commonly sung to a tune called 'Rutherford'. Not all who sing these moving words are aware that they are based on the death-bed sayings of the seventeenth century Scottish preacher, Samuel Rutherford. Only about six verses appear in most hymn books but the original poem contained nineteen stanzas. Its lines also weave in much of the imagery and often the actual words found in the *Letters of Samuel Rutherford* and are very beautiful.

I have known and loved this poem for many years but the seed-thought for this small volume came from a nineteenth century biography of Rutherford by Andrew Thomson. In a discussion on the qualities of Rutherford's unique letters Thomson maintains that many are already poetry in all but form. He then suggests that 'a skilful versifier in sympathy with the author' could easily turn many of the letters into poems and so enrich the universal Church. This I have attempted to do. The work and thought involved have proved a great blessing to me, and it is my prayer that through these pages Samuel Rutherford may again bring the consolations of God to Christian men and women facing the temptations and trials of life.

FAITH COOK
November 1988

CONTENTS

Samuel Rutherford   15
    A Pastor's Prayer
    Wrestling to Believe
    The Exiled Pastor
    Heaven on Earth
    Christ Altogether Lovely

Lady Kenmure   27
    The Thorny Hedge
    God's Strange Ways
    True Consolation
    The End of the Journey
    Past Finding Out
    Christ Shares His People's Sorrows
    God's Purposes in Trial
    The Pilgrim Path
    The Last River
    Fruits of Glory

Lady Boyd   42
    Joy and Sorrow
    The Presence of Christ
    Anticipation of Heaven
    Immanuel's Land
    A Prayer for Revival

Marion M'Naught   51
    Unforgotten Prayers

John Gordon of Cardoness   55
    Earnest Entreaties with a Friend
    Stray Affections

William Gordon of Earlston   60
    A Prisoner of Hope

Lady Culross   63
    An Absent Christ
    The Banished Pastor's Consolation

Lady Robertland   67
    Christ's Secret Gate

John Kennedy of Ayr   69
    Die Well

George Gillespie   73
    To a Dying Friend

Robert Gordon of Knockbrex   77
    The Trial of Grace

Alexander Gordon of Knockgray   79
    When Christ Comes

John Gordon at Rusco   82
    This Vain World

Other Correspondents   86
    Christ's Rough Serjeants
    Through Brier and Bush
    For Me to Live is Christ
    The Greatest Temptation

ILLUSTRATIONS

		Facing page
1	'Wood, trees, meadows and hills' of Anwoth (see page 16).	16
2	Cardoness Castle, just over a mile from Anwoth (see page 16).	17
3	Drum Castle, near Aberdeen, where Rutherford was exiled (see page 17).	32
4	Old Anwoth Church: 'There I wrestled with the Angel and prevailed' (see page 21).	33
5	'The rose is neighbour to the thorn' (see page 45).	48
6	'I can but wait upon the bank until God's wind shall blow'(see page 46).	49
7	Kirkcudbright across the River Dee, home of Marion M'Naught, Rutherford's principal correspondent (see page 51).	64
8	The banks of Loch Ken. Kenmure Castle is hidden among trees in the background (see page 73).	65

Photographs 1, 2, 4, 7 and 8 are by A W Medley, photograph 6 by G J Hanwell and photograph 5 by P H Stubbs to all of whom grateful acknowledgement is made.

ACKNOWLEDGMENTS

All quotations and letter references are taken from the Bonar edition of the *Letters of Samuel Rutherford*, republished in 1984 by the Banner of Truth Trust.

SAMUEL RUTHERFORD

Far removed as the days of the Scottish Covenanters may seem from the scene of twentieth-century Christianity, a careful study of the *Letters of Samuel Rutherford*, which were collected and published shortly after his death in 1661, will reward the reader with fascinating insights into the spiritual experiences of men and women of another generation. It can also lead us into a deeper understanding of the ways of God towards His people which are unchanging from age to age.

Samuel Rutherford was born in the year 1600 in the little village of Nisbet near Jedburgh, and in this rural part of the Scottish Borders he and his brothers, James and George, grew to manhood. The exceptional abilities of this farmer's lad were soon evident and in the year 1617 he took up studies in Edinburgh. In 1621 he obtained his Master of Arts degree and two years later was appointed Professor of Humanity, only retaining this post for a short time before giving it up in 1625 to engage in private studies prior to his entry into the Christian ministry.

Young Samuel Rutherford was probably twenty-four years of age before he received the light of the Gospel into his mind and found 'the excellence, sweetness and beauty of that high and lofty One, Christ' gripping his affections. 'Like a fool as I was', he grieves in a letter to Robert Stuart of Ayr, 'I suffered my sun to be high in the heaven, and near afternoon, before ever I took the gate by the end' (Letter 186). His home village of Nisbet was one of the numerous villages in the land where a man might live out his days without any opportunity to hear of Christ. Writing of Nisbet in later years Rutherford describes it as a place 'in which I fear Christ was scarce named' (Letter 344).

In 1627 Rutherford accepted an invitation from Sir John Gordon of Lochinvar – later to become Lord Kenmure – to the newly-formed parish of Anwoth. So began a ministry in this quiet corner of south-west Scotland lasting only nine years and yet one which has set the name of Anwoth for ever in the hearts of Christian people. 'Fair Anwoth by the Solway' became the dearest spot on earth to Samuel Rutherford and here he gave himself to incessant labours among the people.

It is not hard to imagine the old manse at Bush o'Bield – now gone without a trace – and the little copse of trees separating the house from the church. Rutherford's candle often burnt late into the night as he bowed over his studies and it was his practice to rise at three o'clock in the morning to hold communion with his Saviour. Again and again he was to be found pacing up and down his tree-lined path pouring out his soul to God and imploring the aid of His Spirit in his preaching. The path became known as Rutherford's Walk. In later years he could call on the woods and hills of Galloway to bear witness to the earnest supplications that he had sent heavenward as he sought to 'draw on a fair meeting betwixt Christ and Anwoth' (Letter 279; see poem, *A Pastor's Prayer*).

Rutherford's preaching began to arrest attention in all the surrounding neighbourhood and the little church was soon crowded to capacity. Although his voice was rather shrill and not easy to listen to, this was quickly forgotten as he gripped the hearts of his hearers. Wodrow in his *Church History* describes him as 'one of the most moving and affectionate preachers in his time or perhaps any age of the Church'. Marion M'Naught, wife of the Provost of Kirkcudbright, was only one of many who found their steps irresistibly drawn to Anwoth where the small fair-haired preacher lifted their eyes away from the cheerless scenes of daily life and showed them the loveliness of Christ.

A passionate concern for the people characterized Rutherford's ministry, and he dealt plainly and earnestly with peasant and noble alike. Lord Kenmure's spiritual condition was a cause of much anxiety for it seemed that love of worldly honour had captivated his heart, while Lady Kenmure's great sufferings and godliness drew out his warmest affections and pastoral care. The tough old laird of Cardoness Castle, John Gordon, was an object of his continual prayers and to him he could write, 'Thoughts of your soul . . . depart not from me in my sleep . . . Oh, if I could buy your soul's salvation with any suffering whatsoever, that ye and I might meet with joy up in the rainbow, when we shall stand before our Judge' (Letter 180).

During his Anwoth days Rutherford learnt through much affliction to be a compassionate pastor to Christ's flock. Both his children died in infancy and in 1630 his young wife Eupham also died after a year of most distressing illness. Words penned to Marion M'Naught reveal the anguish of his heart: 'My wife is so sore tormented night and day, that I have wondered why the Lord

[16]

1 'Wood, trees, meadows and hills' of Anwoth.

2   Cardoness Castle, just over a mile from Anwoth.

tarrieth so long. My life is bitter unto me . . . it is hard to keep sight of God in a storm' (Letter 6). Shortly after Eupham's death Rutherford, worn with sorrow and overwork, fell ill himself and Marion M'Naught sent her daughter Grizzel from Kirkcudbright to care for him.

With a ministry such as Rutherford was exercising in the troubled days of Charles I, it was inevitable that sooner or later he would draw down the wrath of the religious authorities who wished to re-establish episcopacy in the Scottish Churches. Rutherford had published a book exposing the errors of Archbishop Laud, Charles I's right-hand man, and he could see the storm-clouds gathering. Writing to Lady Kenmure early in 1636 he says, 'I hang by a thread, but it is (if I may speak so) of Christ's spinning' (Letter 56). Rutherford was right; in July of that year he faced a farcical trial, first at Wigtown and then in Edinburgh. He was forbidden to preach in any part of Scotland and banished to Aberdeen to await the King's decision concerning him.

On an Autumn morning in 1636 a sorrowful little party could be seen standing near the approaches to the old town of Aberdeen. It was a small group of men and women from Anwoth saying a last farewell to Samuel Rutherford, their pastor. They had travelled two hundred and twenty miles with him from the slopes of Galloway to this stern northern fortress. Although Rutherford had bravely declared that his place of exile would be 'Christ's palace' to him and expressed the confidence that Christ would make Aberdeen, 'my garden of delights', it was with heavy hearts they finally parted. So began the hardest and yet most spiritually fruitful period of Rutherford's life, for from his lonely exile flowed at least two hundred letters to friends and members of his Anwoth flock – letters that have caused his name to be known and loved ever since. Through these Rutherford was to become a son of consolation to countless generations of Christians passing through the sorrows and trials of their earthly pathway.

Bereaved of his family, his preaching had become his 'poor man's one eye'. In great desolation he now exclaims: 'Next to Christ, I had but one joy, the apple of the eye of my delights, to preach Christ my Lord; and they have violently plucked that away from me' (Letter 225). During his early months in Aberdeen Rutherford struggled against much dejection of spirit and a fear that his banishment was a mark of divine displeasure. Some of his letters reflect this heaviness when he confides to Marion M'Naught: 'That day that my mouth was most unjustly and cruelly closed, the bloom fell off my branches, and my joy did cast the flower . . . my faith hath bowed . . . under this almost insupportable weight! Oh that it break not' (Letter 185; see poem, *Wrestling to Believe*).

Above all else a concern for his needy flock distressed Rutherford's pastor-heart and his letters to Anwoth are filled with tenderness and anxiety. 'My day-thoughts and my night-thoughts are of you:', he writes; 'while ye sleep I am afraid of your souls . . . My witness is above; your heaven would be two heavens to me, and the salvation of you all as two salvations to me' (Letter 225; see poem, *The Exiled Pastor*).

If his sorrows were great so also were his consolations. His letters throb with the praise of Christ, and he continually exhorts his correspondents to join him in exalting his royal Master who had allowed him the privilege of suffering for His sake. It is clear that Christ favoured His servant with rare and extraordinary experiences of His love so that he could write to John Nevay: 'I find that my extremity hath sharpened the edge of His love and kindness, so that He seemeth to divise new ways of expressing the sweetness of His love to my soul . . . Nay, but I find that it is possible to find young glory, and a young green paradise of joy, even here' (Letter 179; see poem, *Heaven on Earth*).

The outstanding theme of these letters is the majesty and loveliness of Christ; all the passion and poetry latent in Rutherford's soul springs to life as he describes his well-beloved Saviour:

'Oh, but Christ is heaven's wonder, and earth's wonder! What marvel that His bride saith, "He is altogether lovely!" . . . Oh, pity for evermore, that there should be such a one as Christ Jesus, so boundless, so bottomless, and so incomparable in infinite excellency and sweetness, and so few to take Him'.

(Letter 226; see poem, *Christ Altogether Lovely*)

The signing of the National Covenant in March 1638 and the scenes of revival that followed, brought a sharp turn in the affairs of Church and State. Rutherford took advantage of the weakened position of the episcopal party to risk the fury of the law and to discharge himself from his exile. In June he returned to his manse in Anwoth and though there was neither wife nor child to greet his return, gladness spread through the homes of nobleman and villager alike. But the joy was shortlived: only a year later the Assembly of the Church of Scotland confirmed its wish that Rutherford move to St Andrews and fill the strategic position of Professor of Divinity at St Mary's College.

Rutherford grieved anew over this separation and expressed his feelings to Lady Kenmure: 'My removal from my flock is so heavy to me, that it maketh my life a burden to me . . . The Lord help and hold up sad clay' (Letter 287). But he was compelled to yield to God's unmistakable will and in October 1639 left Anwoth for the last time. Rutherford was eminently fitted for this new work, and his removal from the Galloway area ensured that letters would continue to flow from his ready pen: to Lady Kenmure, to Alexander Gordon of Earlston, to Lady Boyd and to many others whose needs weighed upon his heart. After five months at St Andrews, Rutherford, who had been a widower for ten years, married Jean McMath, 'a woman or rare worth and spirit' to use the words of an early biographer.

Rutherford lived in turbulent and epoch-making days in the history of Christ's Church, and it was not long before his outstanding abilities were further called upon. In 1643 he was chosen as one of four main Scottish representatives appointed to go up to London to take part in formulating the famous Westminster Confession of Faith. Alongside the most eminent of England's godly and gifted ministers he laboured for four years until the Confession was completed in 1647.

Before he went to London two children were born to Rutherford from his second marriage, but during his period there he and his wife laid both these little ones in early graves so that Rutherford returned once more to a childless home. He writes sorrowfully of this to another bereaved parent, 'I had but two children, and both are dead since I came hither . . . The good Husbandman may pluck His roses, and gather in His lilies at mid-summer, and, for aught I dare say, in the beginning of the first summer month' (Letter 310).

Samuel Rutherford remained at St Andrews as Professor of Divinity for the rest of his life in spite of attempts by other institutions of learning to acquire his services. With the restoration of Charles II to the throne in 1660 the storm-clouds gathered once more and Rutherford became a marked man. This was due mainly to his far-sighted and controversial work, *Lex Rex*, which he published in 1644. In this book he argued closely and forcefully against the arbitrary and tyrannical rule of the monarch. In September 1660 the Committee of Estates examined the treatise and then declared the possession of the book an act of treason. Copies were publicly burnt both in Edinburgh and St Andrews.

Rutherford was singled out for destruction together with three more of Scotland's most distinguished sons. The Marquis of Argyll, Lady Kenmure's brother, was executed in May 1661, James Guthrie faced the scaffold in June of that same year, and Archibald Johnstone escaped temporarily by taking refuge on the Continent. When the Commissioners arrived from London bearing the summons for Rutherford's arrest he was already dying. Told of their arrival his sunken eyes lit up with their old fire, and taking the document into his frail hand he said imperiously, 'Tell them that I have a summons already from a superior Judge . . . and ere your day arrive, I will be where few kings and great folks come.'

For long years Rutherford had waited for the day when he should see his 'kingly King': 'Oh, how long it is to the dawning of the marriage day!', he would cry. . . . 'Oh, if He would fold the heavens together like an old cloak, and shovel time and days out of the way, and make ready in haste the Lamb's wife for her Husband' (Letter 180)! Now he stood on the very borders of 'Immanuel's Land'. Many waited around that death-bed to catch his dying words. Also waiting there was one little girl, Agnes, only surviving child of the seven born to him by his second wife. Looking at his eleven-year old daughter he said simply, 'I have left her upon the Lord'. Repeatedly he was heard to call for 'a well-tuned harp', longing already to join the anthems of praise above. On the last afternoon of his life, with strange foresight, he was able to say: 'This night will close the door and fasten my anchor within the veil, and I shall go away in a sleep by five in the morning.' And so he did. His last recorded words were, 'Glory, glory dwelleth in Immanuel's Land', and as dawn broke on March 29th 1661, night was gone forever for Samuel Rutherford as he came at last to 'Immanuel's high and blessed land' (Letter 333).

Samuel Rutherford

A PASTOR'S PRAYER

'Pray for my poor flock: . . . I fear that the entering of a hireling upon my labours there will cut off my life with sorrow. There I wrestled with the Angel and prevailed. Wood, trees, meadows and hills are my witnesses that I drew on a fair meeting betwixt Christ and Anwoth.'

Wood and meadows, hills and trees,
Witness bear with me;
Heard you not a pastor's prayer,
Marked his lonely plea;
Bowed beneath a midnight sky
Keeping faithful tryst,
Till I drew a meeting fair
Between my flock and Christ?
With the Angel there I strove,
Strove and did prevail,
Strengthened by the grace of God
That I might not fail.

Still for my poor flock I pray,
Lest the wolf devour
Or some hireling leave the sheep
In a needy hour.
God of pity, hear this plea
Humbly on You cast,
Bring them through a cloudy day
Safely home at last.

TO MARION M'NAUGHT
Aberdeen, November 1637
Letter 279

WRESTLING TO BELIEVE

*'I have been casting myself under God's feet, and wrestling to believe
under a hidden and covered Lord; . . . I dare not say that the Lord
hath put out my candle, and hath casten water upon my poor coal . . .
I had but one joy, and no more, and one green flower that I esteemed
to be my garland, He came in one hour and dried up my flower at the
root . . .'*

Inscrutable the ways of God,
Beyond the mind of man!
For who can read His hidden thought
Or search His secret plan?
I had one joy, one garland fair,
The flower I loved the best,
But in a single hour Christ came
And plucked it to His breast.

I dare not say the Lord has quenched
My candle's flickering glow,
Or cast His waters on the coals
That burnt already low;
And still I wrestle to believe
A veiled and covered God,
But faint my heart, my faith bowed down
Beneath the pressing load.

O that my Lord might smile again,
His love upon me pour;
Come home to this afflicted heart,
Bring summer back once more!
Then would I preach with unloosed tongue
His beauty and His power,
My withered branch would bud anew
And bear another flower.

Yet God in wisdom chose for me
This furnace and this flame,
And doubting not His choice the best,
I greet it in His name.

[22]

Samuel Rutherford

So will I praise Him for this stroke,
Till Christ at length appears
To turn my long captivity
And dry His people's tears.

TO MARION M'NAUGHT
Aberdeen, 1637
Letter 185

THE EXILED PASTOR

*'Next to Christ, I had but one joy, . . . to preach Christ my Lord; . . .
It was to me like the poor man's one eye; and they have put out that
eye, . . . Oh, if any pain, and sorrow, any loss that I can suffer for
Christ and for you were laid in pledge to buy Christ's love to you! . . .
My witness is above; your heaven would be two heavens to me and the
salvation of you all as two salvations to me.'*

Once with earnest heart I preached
God's eternal word;
Dearer this than all to me
Next to Christ my Lord.
But my foes with base intent
Stole that chief delight,
Plucked a poor man's only eye
Robbing him of sight.
Silent am I now and bound
For my princely Lord,
Yet for you my prayers arise,
Ceaselessly outpoured.

Call to mind those days now fled
When with eager tongue
All my Bridegroom's worth I spoke,
His fair glories sung;
Preached of One whose pain and death
Could alone suffice,
Till your hearts made glad reply,
'So I take you, Christ'.

[23]

Freely would I lay in pledge
Sorrow, loss and pain,
Purchase your eternity,
Lest I've preached in vain.
Your salvation is my life,
Christ can witness bear
That my heaven would be two heavens
Could I greet you there.

By the sighs and tears of Christ,
By His wounds and blood,
There together may we feast,
Near the throne of God.

Aberdeen, July 1637
Letter 225

HEAVEN ON EARTH

*'My extremity hath sharpened the edge of His love and kindness . . . I
would desire no more for my heaven . . . while I am sighing in this
house of clay, but daily renewed feasts of love with Christ, and liberty
now and then to feed my hunger with a kiss of that fairest face . . .
Nay, but I find that it is possible to find young glory and a young green
paradise of joy, even here.'*

O child of God, no longer mourn
Supposing you may only know
Affliction, crosses, tears and woe
Until the glory dawn;
For in my sore extremity
Christ spoke His heart of love to me
Till heaven on earth was born.

And could I wish a better heaven
While sighing in this house of clay
Than feasts of love with Christ each day,
And freedom now and then
To feed my hunger with a kiss
Stolen from His fairest face,
My weakness to sustain?

My soul has known a glory here
That pain and loss can not destroy:
A young green paradise of joy
All strewn with flowers rare.
Here I have sipped its springs of love,
Drawn from the fountain-head above,
And breathed its vernal air.

While bound by time to earth and sense,
The heirs of glory may implore
More borrowed joys from heaven's store,
As sorrow's recompense;
And may for nearer union pine,
Till Christ our happy souls assign
A full inheritance.

TO JOHN NEVAY
Aberdeen, June 1637
Letter 179

CHRIST ALTOGETHER LOVELY

'Oh, what a fair One, what an only One, what an excellent, lovely, ravishing One, is Jesus! Put the beauty of ten thousand thousand worlds of paradises, like the garden of Eden in one; . . . And yet it would be less to that fair and dearest Well-beloved, Christ, . . . What heaven can be there liker to hell . . . than to . . . fall a swoon for Christ's love, and to want it? . . . Is not this pain and joy, sweetness and sadness, . . . in one web?'

All-lovely Christ! My pen could never trace
That fairest flower of Paradise!
A glory rests upon His kingly face,
And shines within His eyes.

Let countless Edens blend in harmony,
His beauty still outshines them far,
As massy oceans swallow up a sea
Or sunlight hides the star.

One look from Christ seems half a heaven to me,
One kiss would break my happy heart
And but the meanest share in Him would be
A sinner's welcome part.

To yearn for Christ while still He hides His face
Is like a heaven and hell in one;
An interwoven tapestry of grace
With pain and sweetness spun.

And so through all the thorns of life I press
To grasp Him in a troubled day,
Enfold Him day and night within my breast
Till called from earth away.

TO LADY KILCONQUHAR
Aberdeen, August 1637
Letter 226

LADY KENMURE

Lady Jane Kenmure sat beside her dying husband. Born in 1600 into a noble and distinguished Scottish family, her lot might have been the envy of many, but the path that providence had marked out for this young woman was one of much suffering. She had been married only eight years and already had lost her three little daughters in death.

Lady Jane was the daughter of Archibald Campbell, seventh Earl of Argyll and in 1626 she married Sir John Gordon of Lochinvar who later became Lord Kenmure. Not long after their marriage Sir John had used his considerable influence to secure the services of the young Samuel Rutherford as minister in the newly-formed parish of Anwoth. Anwoth lay about twenty miles from the stately home of Lord and Lady Kenmure, the ruins of which can still be seen nestling among the woods that lie along the shores of the beautiful Loch Ken in Galloway.

Although Lady Jane performed no outstanding deed, and left behind no diaries, letters or memoirs, her name is better known than any other religious lady of the period. It is the pastoral letters she received from Samuel Rutherford – perhaps the most poignant and profound ever penned by this prince of letter-writers – that have immortalized her memory.

From his earliest days in Anwoth Rutherford felt a deep concern for Sir John and his wife. King Charles I, in order to curry favour with some of the Scottish nobility, had conferred honours and titles upon many and in 1633 Sir John had been created Viscount of Kenmure and Lord Gordon of Lochinvar. The lure of worldly advancement and the secret hope of future honours from the King had become a temptation too strong to resist, and Sir John had begun to disregard spiritual values and standards, becoming careless and profane.

Sir John's spiritual condition caused his pastor no little anxiety. 'Stir up your husband', he wrote to Lady Kenmure on one occasion, 'to lay hold upon the covenant . . . What hath he to do with the world?' (Letter 28). A little later he wrote, 'Drop words in the ears of your noble husband continually of eternity, judgment, death, hell, heaven . . .' (Letter 30).

Early in 1629 Lady Kenmure had suffered the loss of her first little daughter. Rutherford wrote to her very tenderly: 'Ye have lost a child: nay she is not lost to you who is found to Christ. She is not sent away, but only sent before, like unto a star, which going out of our sight doth not die . . . but shineth in another hemisphere' (Letter 4; see poem, *The Thorny Hedge*).

Grief was never far away. In 1633 another infant daughter died, and in 1634 she lost a little girl of eighteen months old – her last child. Rutherford showed great concern for Lady Kenmure, and wrote to her friend and relative Marion M'Naught, urging her to visit the bereaved mother, '. . . her child is with the Lord; I entreat you to visit her, for I think she will be heavy'. Meanwhile he penned one of his most beautiful letters which has brought consolation to countless suffering Christians: 'Let the movables go; why not? They are not yours. Fasten your grips upon the heritage; and our Lord Jesus . . . give your Ladyship to grow as a palm-tree on God's Mount Zion; howbeit shaken with winds, yet the root is fast' (Letter 35; see poem, *God's Strange Ways*).

And now in the Autumn of 1634 Sir John himself was dying. No warning from the pen of Samuel Rutherford had awakened his conscience but the approach of death itself caused this time-serving noble to tremble. 'What shall I do', he asked fearfully, 'for I dare not die, howbeit I know I must die, for I find my sins so grievous and so many?' Sir John begged Rutherford to remain with him to the end. God in His mercy came to the dying man, powerfully converting his soul through the words of his faithful pastor. The amazing conversations that took place were written down by Rutherford himself and later published under the title *The Last and Heavenly Speeches of Lord Kenmure*. Never, perhaps, in the long history of the Christian Church, has there been recorded a more moving account of a man in the throes of death wrestling to believe and finding refuge and forgiveness in Christ at the last.

Initially Sir John evidenced many signs of genuine repentance until Rutherford was able to say, 'My Lord, your prayers and tears are come up before God, and Christ hath obtained a pardon for you'. But upon some slight recovery, John Gordon's renewed carelessness of spirit refuted his professions, and Rutherford, with all the rigour of a true pastor, stripped away his supposed confidence and urged his lordship to 'dig deeper', that he might lay a sure foundation for his soul. Then Sir John was stricken with many pangs of conscience and confessed sins of which his pastor was totally ignorant. But there was mercy for Lord Kenmure, and the outstanding sign of a renewed heart in the eyes of Rutherford was the expression of great love to Christ, while still anticipating final rejection on account of his sins. 'Howbeit He should not love me', Sir John declared, 'yet I will still love Him . . . let Him trample on me, I will die if I die at Christ's feet'.

Sir John's remaining days on earth were spent in prayer and meditation, and seeking the forgiveness of those he might have wronged. Just moments before he died his pastor asked, 'Have you any sense of the Lord's love?' 'I have', replied the dying man. 'And will you part with Him?' persisted Rutherford tenderly, 'By no means', came back the low reply, and these words were his last. As Rutherford prayed it was noticed that Sir John was 'joyfully smiling, and looking up with glorious looks'. As the last "Amen" of that prayer was spoken he died and Christ crowned him with the nobler accolades of heaven.

Following this event Rutherford wrote two moving letters to his bereaved friend, Lady Kenmure. 'I thought', he writes in one, 'our Lord brake the sharp point off the cross, . . . I know the sweetest of it is bitter to you; . . . Only, Madam, God commandeth you now to believe and cast anchor in the dark night, and climb up the mountain' (Letter 39; see poem, *True Consolation*).

Just a month or two after the death of her husband, Lady Kenmure gave birth to a son and it is not hard to imagine that all her devotion was heaped upon this child. Rutherford feared for her, lest she should lose him as well, and continually pointed her to the eternal heritage. 'He . . . hath left little to woo your love from Himself, except one only child . . . Look to the east, the day sky is breaking' (Letter 56); and again, 'Let your child be Christ's; let him stay beside you as thy Lord's pledge that you shall willingly render again, if God will' (Letter 69; see poem, *The End of the Journey*).

Throughout Rutherford's confinement in Aberdeen during 1636 and 1637, he continued to correspond with Lady Kenmure. His ability to pour out some of his most intimate and exalted experiences of Christ to her speaks much for the spiritual life of his correspondent (See poem, *Past Finding Out*).

In 1639 Rutherford's fears turned to reality for Lady Kenmure's little son John sickened and died at the age of four. Even Rutherford was staggered at this sorrow and says, 'I confess it seemed strange to me, that your Lord should have done that which seemed to ding out the bottom of your worldly comforts'. In a letter revealing the depth of his pastoral concern, he acknowledges her grief which, he says, '. . . will have its own violent incursions in your soul: and I think it be not in your power to help it . . . Madam, I would that I could divide sorrow with you . . . But I am but a beholder; . . . the God of comfort speak to you, and allure you with His feasts of love' (Letter 287; see poem, *Christ Shares His People's Sorrows*).

About a year after this Lady Kenmure remarried. Her second husband, Sir Henry Montgomery, was a man whose spiritual interests were most compatible with those of his wife; Rutherford describes him as 'an active and faithful friend of the Lord's kirk.' But this happiness, too, was short-lived for Sir Henry died soon afterwards and Lady Kenmure must have recalled the words of Rutherford: 'He [Christ] seeketh his answer of you in affliction, to see if ye will say, "Even so I take Him"' (Letter 20; see poem, *God's Purposes in Trial*).

Rutherford's letters contain many allusions to his friend's ill-health, but she outlived him and his death in 1661 must have left her bereft indeed. Lady Kenmure lived on to a considerable age, though little is known of her later years; but as she reviewed her life, and the sorrows of her pathway, she must surely have recollected words that Samuel Rutherford had written to her many years before:

'Madam . . . when ye are got up thither, and have cast your eyes to view the golden city, and the fair and never-withering Tree of Life . . . ye shall then say, "Four-and-twenty hours' abode in this place is worth threescore and ten years' sorrow upon earth"'.
(Letter 19; see poems, *The Pilgrim Path* and *The Last River*)

Lady Kenmure

THE THORNY HEDGE

*'Build your nest upon no tree here; for ye see God hath sold the forest
to death; and every tree whereupon we would rest is ready to be cut
down . . . The hedge of thorns . . . which God buildeth in your way,
to hinder you from this lover, [i.e. the world] is the thorny hedge of
daily grief . . . What lose ye, if God twist and plait the hedge daily
thicker?'*

From tender years your way has been
Through flood and furnace cast
The patient form of Christ to stamp
Upon your soul at last.

A thorny hedge of daily grief
Is set across your way:
Of weakness, loss, uncertainty,
Or fear's oppressive sway.
What matters it if God should weave
The hedge more thickly yet,
Lest you look back on wayward years
With lingering vain regret.

A little child is lost to you,
(How short her hour-glass here!)
Yet all she lacked of time is gained
In heaven's unbroken year.
And can a child be lost indeed
Whom Christ has sought and found?
Though poorer here, with lasting wealth
Your heaven shall abound.

This forest God has sold to death
So build not here your nest,
For every tree shall be hewn down
Where you might seek to rest.
The grains of sand in time's short glass
Are less than yesterday,
Its ever-posting span of hours
Refuses long to stay.

As watchmen wait and long for dawn,
And gaze with weary eyes,
So watch till Christ's fair morning breaks
Across the eastern skies.

TO LADY KENMURE
On the death of her infant daughter
Anwoth, January 1629
Letter 4

GOD'S STRANGE WAYS

'I believe faith will teach you to kiss a striking Lord; . . . If our dear Lord pluck up one of His roses, and pull down sour and green fruit before harvest, who can challenge Him? . . . Your Husbandman and Lord hath lopped off some branches already; . . . All these crosses . . . are to make you white and ripe for the Lord's harvest-hook.'

Though strange may seem God's ways
Your hasty lips refrain,
For here we see but broken links
Of glory's perfect chain.

The Husbandman of heaven
His tree may freely prune,
So challenge not His ways or say
He cut this branch too soon.
By wounding and by loss
He seeks pure fruit at last;
Though shaken now by storm and wind
Yet still the root is fast.

3　Drum Castle, near Aberdeen, where Rutherford was exiled.

4   Old Anwoth Church.

Lady Kenmure

And if the Lord's fair hand
Should pluck a little rose,
Or harvest green mid-summer fruit
Ere sweet and ripe it grows,
Then meekly own His right,
And Christ will grace afford,
Till faith has taught your weeping heart
To kiss a striking Lord.

Should time's best comforts die
The heritage remains;
Hold fast in faith till Christ transplants
His tree to sunnier plains.

TO LADY KENMURE
On the death of her daughter
Anwoth, April 1634
Letter 35

TRUE CONSOLATION

'This world never looked like a friend upon you: Ye owe it little love. It looked ever sour-like upon you. Howbeit ye should woo it, it will not match with you; and therefore never seek warm fire under cold ice. This is not a field where your happiness groweth; it is up above.'

A heavy portion Christ has weighed
A pressing burden early laid
Upon your youthful back;
For you must walk each day alone
Bereft of one who has out-flown
The restless shores of time.
There he exults in realms sublime
While you but glimpse his track.
And Christ too seems to hide His face
Yet will He turn with warm embrace
To heal the bruisèd heart.

No friend has this world been to you,
And while its charms you vainly woo,
It frowns upon you still.
Then loose your grip on transient things
That fly with time's evasive wings
Or die like fire in ice.
True friend and lover seek in Christ
Who waits your arms to fill.
In heavenly scenes your joys must grow
Far from these fields of mortal woe,
This vale of grief and tears.

God's chastening hand you long have known
To fashion you a fair carved stone
Fit for His courts on high.
Though painted joys of earth may go
Far better gifts will Christ bestow:
A heritage secure,
A home that changeless shall endure
Where joys can never die.
And should all friends from hence remove
The pent-up flood-tides of your love
On Christ alone be poured.

TO LADY KENMURE
On the death of her husband
Anwoth, September 1634
Letter 37

Lady Kenmure

THE END OF THE JOURNEY

*'You have reason to take in good part a lean dinner and spare diet in this
life, seeing your large supper of the Lamb's preparing will recompense
all . . . Look to the east, the day sky is breaking. Think not that Christ
loseth time, or lingereth unsuitably.'*

Look to the east for the day sky is breaking
Soon shall the winter of sorrow be past;
Christ lingers not, nor delays in His coming,
Warm are the rays of His dawning at last.

Stormy this life and its billows tempestuous,
Gladly our anchor we cast in the veil;
Many make ship-wreck and sink in deep waters,
Better to swim in the teeth of the gale!

Long since this world has forsaken, despised you,
Few are the comforts that lighten your way;
Quicken your steps to salute His appearing,
Grey-headed Time bids you hasten away.

Fetch home to Christ every wayward affection,
Pour at His feet the full measure of love,
Patiently bear with life's scanty lean diet:
Christ is preparing a banquet above!

Look on in hope to the end of the journey,
Far though your feet in the desert may roam;
Eagerly Christ is awaiting His loved ones,
Granting the pilgrim a sweet welcome home.

TO LADY KENMURE
Anwoth, January 1636
Letter 56

PAST FINDING OUT

'There are curtains to be drawn by in Christ, that we never saw, and new foldings of love in Him. I despair that ever I shall win to the far end of that love, there are so many plies in it . . . His love surroundeth and surchargeth me. I am burdened with it; but oh, how sweet and lovely is that burden! . . . I am so in love with His love, that if His love were not in heaven, I should be unwilling to go thither.'

The love of Christ!
Far, far beyond my finite mind,
Past finding out to mortal man;
Though searching still, I yet despair
Its farthest bounds to span.

O hidden love!
A curtain veils Christ's secret heart
That none can ever fully draw,
With fold on fold of unseen depths
I scarcely knew before.

But now at length,
With pressure of exquisite joy,
That love surrounds and burdens me
Until my soul can hardly bear
The weight of ecstasy.

Sweet love of Christ!
Revealed in part yet hidden still,
Unsearchable, but strangely near;
And heaven would not be heaven to me
Unless His love were there!

TO LADY KENMURE
Aberdeen, March 1637
Letter 104

Lady Kenmure

CHRIST SHARES HIS PEOPLE'S SORROWS

'Subscribe to the Almighty's will; put your hand to the pen, and let the cross of your Lord Jesus have your submissive and resolute AMEN . . . I shall believe, for my part, that He mindeth to distil heaven out of this loss, and all others the like; for wisdom devised it, and love laid it on, and Christ owneth it as His own, and putteth your shoulder beneath only a piece of it . . .'

O child of God this grief
That bows your spirit low
Is yours but half, for Christ Himself
Still shares His people's woe.

His wisdom planned it out
Then bore it on His heart
Till gently on your untried back
Love laid the lesser part.

So take it all with joy,
Together bear the cross,
For while you suffer He distils
A heaven from your loss.

Beneath His secret will
Subscribe with ready pen,
Add to this sorrow God has sent
A resolute 'Amen'.

Each day spend out in faith,
Nor prove His labour vain;
Cast still on Christ the pressing weight
Who only can sustain.

TO LADY KENMURE
On the death of her son
October 1639
Letter 287

GOD'S PURPOSES IN TRIAL

'God aimeth, in all His dealings with His children, to bring them to a high contempt of, and deadly feud with the world . . . And for no other cause . . . doth the Lord withdraw from you the childish toys and the earthly delights that He giveth unto others, but that He may have you wholly to Himself.'

God aims in all His ways
To bring His children here
To view this world with high contempt
Not worth a passing tear.

He seeks your unshared love
And for no other cause
Your Lord removes time's short delights,
Its childish toys withdraws.

For from affliction's cup
Love's sweetest fragrance flows;
No tree more angry than the thorn
Yet from it springs the rose.

As new-born princes weep,
Heedless of crown or throne,
So heaven's heirs, distressed forget
The heritage they own.

To know sweet comforts now
In frequent prayer be found,
For there your faith may kiss your Lord,
His love embrace you round.

TO LADY KENMURE
Anwoth, 1632
Letter 20

Lady Kenmure

THE PILGRIM PATH

'It is your part now to believe, and suffer, and hope, and wait on . . . I would not want the sweet experience of the consolations of God for all the bitterness of affliction. Nay, whether God come to His children with a rod or a crown, if He come Himself with it, it is well. Welcome, welcome, Jesus, what way soever Thou come, if we can get a sight of Thee! . . .'

When on eternity's fair shore
I stand at last and looking back
May trace the pilgrim path I trod,
The toilsome track,

Then shall I see through glory's glass
How right the way, the path how wise
That led through desert, wind and storm
To this great prize.

From that clear height I then shall say,
'Had God dealt otherwise than this,
What consolations would I know,
Or crown of bliss?'

Then welcome, welcome, lovely Lord,
Come though it be with smile or frown,
Come if it be with smarting rod
Or yet a crown.

But only come: my comfort here
To glimpse that face as bright as morn;
So let me suffer, hope and wait
Till glory dawn.

TO LADY KENMURE
June 1630
Letter 11

THE LAST RIVER

'Be content to wade through the waters betwixt you and glory with Him, holding His hand fast, for He knoweth all the fords . . . weary not; . . . when ye are got up thither, . . . ye shall then say, "Four-and-twenty hours' abode in this place is worth threescore and ten years' sorrow upon earth."'

Hold fast the hand of Christ and fearless wade
This last deep river that must cross your way;
Though frail should seem your grip, be undismayed,
He knows the fords and He will be your stay.
You cannot drown for Christ has gone before
To set us stepping stones amid the flood;
Through death and anguish to the farther shore
The path to glory He has marked in blood.

Then calm each fear, nor let your lips complain,
For one short day on heaven's shore is worth
Each tear, each loss, each shaft of secret pain
In seventy years of sorrow here on earth.
With patient hope more firmly grasp His hand
Until your feet shall gain the heavenly land.

TO LADY KENMURE
November 1631
Letter 19

Lady Kenmure

FRUITS OF GLORY

*'That sum of glory will take you and all the angels telling . . . where
every berry and grape . . . beareth no worse fruit than glory, fulness of
joy, and pleasures that endure for evermore! . . . It is need, not virtue,
to be sojourners in a prison; to weep and sigh, and, alas! to sin sixty or
seventy years in a land of tears. The fruits that grow here are all
seasoned and salted with sin.'*

Fair glory land! No tongue can tell
Those hidden wonders that excel
The utmost praise
That angels raise.
A land no wealth can ever buy,
A land where pleasures satisfy.

Blest summer land whose every tree
Bears fruit of endless ecstasy;
Fulness of joy
Without alloy!
A little foretaste now and then
Would soon my fainting heart sustain.

For here we strive full seventy years,
As prisoners in a land of tears;
And fruits that grow
Amid earth's woe
Are seasoned all and marred by sin,
And hard it is a heaven to win.

Though rough the way, the home how fair,
For Christ, the Prince of joy, is there;
No sin can blight
That pure delight,
For we shall see His kingly face
And taste perennial fruits of grace.

TO LADY KENMURE
London, January 1646
Letter 318

[41]

LADY BOYD

A solitary candle burned into the night at Ardross Castle, for even though all the busy household had retired to bed, Lady Boyd was still writing up her diary. This was not a diary of the common gossip and activities of a day but, as John Livingstone tells us in his fascinating account of many of his religious contemporaries, 'Lady Boyd used every night to write what had been the state of her soul all day and what she had observed of the Lord's doing.' The diary is lost and we shall never know in any detail the dealings of God with Lady Boyd, but the ten letters addressed to her by Samuel Rutherford give many hints of the spiritual treasure it must have contained.

Christian Hamilton, born about 1580, was the only daughter of Sir Thomas Hamilton of Priestfield, a capable lawyer, who distinguished himself at the bar by his talent, and was created Lord President of the Court of Session. Her first husband, Robert, ninth Lord Lindsay of Byres, died in 1616 leaving her with two children. A year later, however, she married Sir Robert Boyd and seven children were born to them. Lord Boyd died after only eleven years of marriage and we can only guess at the sorrow and need into which Lady Boyd was plunged.

Like the Countess of Huntington a century later, Lady Boyd used her position and wealth in the service of Christ and took particular pleasure in giving material assistance to the Lord's faithful servants. She was on friendly terms with some of the most eminent ministers of the day and Robert Blair, Robert Bruce, John Livingstone and Samuel Rutherford were among those who spoke of Lady Boyd with the highest esteem.

Lady Boyd was a woman of deeply sensitive conscience and night by night as she recorded the work of God in her soul she was often sorely perplexed both by the corruptions that were still latent within her and by the unexplained ways of God towards her. Although the letters that she wrote to Samuel Rutherford are lost, her problems and questionings drew out his pastor's heart and he writes, 'Now, Madam, for your Ladyship's case', and then goes on to deal tenderly and honestly with the painful problems of her Christian warfare. 'Be sorry at corruption, and be not secure' [i.e. complacent], he advises; but knowing her tendency to self-condemnation adds, '. . . He delighteth to take up fallen bairns, and to mend broken brows. Binding up of wounds is His office . . . The sea-sick passenger shall come to land; Christ will be the first to meet you on the shore' (Letter 107).

Lady Boyd was often troubled because she experienced so little of the felt presence of Christ. In spite of her longings divine visits to her soul seemed only fleeting. Rutherford applied himself to this problem both by recounting his own experiences and by observing the nature of God's ways. 'And for Christ's joyful coming and going, which your Ladyship speaketh of . . . Christ will have joy and sorrow halvers [sharers] of the life of the saints . . . But if sorrow be the greedier halver of our days here, I know that joy's day shall dawn' (Letter 245; see poem, *Joy and Sorrow*). Rutherford confides to her the often-troubled state of his own heart with disarming honesty: 'At home and within I find much black work, and great cause of a low sail, and of little boasting'. Even Rutherford knew periods of spiritual desertion and complains to Lady Boyd: 'I have not now, of a long time, found such high spring-tides as formerly. The sea is out, the wind of His Spirit calm . . .' But he is able to see some blessing even in the absence of Christ and continues, 'Yet sorrow for His absence is sweet; and sighs, with "Saw ye Him whom my soul loveth?" have their own delights' (Letter 277; see poem, *The Presence of Christ*).

Lady Boyd met with many afflictions in life. She faced the grief of being twice widowed and left to bring up her nine children alone. In 1640 a tragic incident occurred in which three of her brothers and other close relatives were killed when Dunglass Castle, which they were defending against the invading English forces, was accidentally blown up. Rutherford writes to console her but also warns her of the danger of attributing such happenings to any other cause but God. 'It is impossible to be submissive . . . if ye stay your thoughts down among the confused rollings and wheels of second causes; as, "Oh the place!" "Oh the time!" "Oh if this had been, this had not followed! . . ." Look up to the master-motion and the first wheel' (Letter 299). It was only three months after this that young Robert Boyd, who had given many early indications of zeal for God and His cause, died of a fever at the age of twenty-four. Often must Lady Boyd have looked with longing to the land where there is no more sorrow or crying; and Rutherford shares with his friend his own homesickness for heaven: 'O time, time, go swiftly, and hasten that day! Sweet Lord

Jesus post! come . . . It is a painful battle for a soul sick of love to fight with absence and delays' (Letter 167; see poem, *Anticipation of Heaven*).

Lady Boyd had not long to wait. Only a few years after, in 1646, Christ called this pilgrim home. Her funeral was conducted by Robert Trail, who had frequently visited her during her last illness. Many members of the Scottish Parliament, then in session at St Andrews, remained in town to pay their last respects to this honourable woman. Samuel Rutherford was in London at the time, but on hearing of his friend's death he wrote these beautiful words to her daughter:

'She is now above the winter, with a little change of place, not of a Saviour; only she enjoyeth Him now without messages, and in His own immediate presence, from whom she heard by letters and messengers before . . . Ye may easily judge, Madam, what a large recompense is made to all her service, her walking with God, and her sorrows, with the first cast of the soul's eye upon the shining and admirably beautiful face of the Lamb.'

(Letter 321; see poem, *Immanuel's Land*)

Lady Boyd

JOY AND SORROW

'*Christ will have joy and sorrow halvers of the life of the saints . . . as the night and the day are kindly partners and halvers of time . . . But if sorrow be the greedier halver of our days here, I know that joy's day shall dawn . . . When we are over the water, Christ shall cry down crosses, and up heaven . . . and down sin, and down sorrow! and up glory . . . up joy for evermore! In this hope, I sleep quietly in Christ's bosom . . .*'

As God in wisdom has ordained
That night and day should ever be
The kindly partners of our time,
So Christ has planned in love for me
That pain and joy my days divide,
Sorrow and peace dwell side by side.
Should sorrow claim the greater share
I wait till joy's glad day shall dawn;
Earth's best is marred by sin, and here
The rose is neighbour to the thorn.
Then let Christ weave life's fabric still,
With dark and light, with good and ill.

My hope will not be put to shame,
For when I reach a heavenly shore
Then Christ shall cry down death and grief
And cry up glory evermore!
In this sure confidence I rest
And sweetly sleep on Jesu's breast.

TO LADY BOYD
Aberdeen, September 1637
Letter 245

THE PRESENCE OF CHRIST

'I have not now, of a long time, found such high spring-tides as formerly. The sea is out, the wind of His Spirit calm; and I cannot buy a wind, or, by requesting the sea, cause it to flow again; only I wait on upon the banks . . . till the Lord send a full sea . . . Yet sorrow for His absence is sweet; and sighs, with "Saw ye Him whom my soul loveth?" have their own delights.'

My sea is out, the Spirit's wind is still,
And desolate the shore;
Those high spring-tides I used to know
I long to know once more.
I cannot buy a wind and it is vain
To beg the tide to flow;
I can but wait upon the bank
Until God's wind shall blow.

A house I build of pining strong desire
To find my absent Lord;
Yet sorrow has its own delights
And pain can joy afford.
I spin a web of hopeful sighs and tears,
My dreams of Him are sweet,
For ere He left, He pledged His love –
A token till we meet.

As misty dews may cheer the drooping flower
Athirst for gentle rain,
So Christ with secret dews of grace
My heart shall still sustain.
But when He comes to flood the waiting soul
With love's full flowing tide,
He bursts the banks with streams of grace,
And I am satisfied.

TO LADY BOYD
Aberdeen, 1637
Letter 277

Lady Boyd

ANTICIPATION OF HEAVEN

*'When He bloweth a kiss afar off to His poor heart-broken mourners in
Zion . . . I am confounded with wonder to think what it shall be, when
the Fairest among the sons of men shall lay a King's sweet soft cheek to
the sinful cheeks of poor sinners. O time, time, go swiftly, and hasten
that day! Sweet Lord Jesus, post! come.'*

O time speed swiftly on,
Bring near the longed-for day
When Christ shall call His mourners here
To come away.

If but a kiss from far
Should be so passing sweet,
What will it be when I shall rise
My Prince to greet?

To see His royal face,
To rest my cheek on His,
To know my vileness cleansed away
What grace is this!

My soul with absence burns
It battles with delay
Could I but hear that glad, 'I come'
How blest the day!

Fair land where Jesus reigns
Dear long-awaited home!
Speed swiftly time, O haste the day,
Lord Jesus, come!

TO LADY BOYD
May 1637
Letter 167

IMMANUEL'S LAND

*'In . . . a land which hath more than four summers in the year. Oh,
what spring-time is there! Even the smelling of . . . that great and
eternally blooming Rose of Sharon for ever and ever! What a singing
life is there! There is not a dumb bird in all that large field; but all sing
and breathe out heaven, joy, glory, dominion to the high Prince of that
new-found land.'*

Immanuel's Land! how high, how fair!
A land of summers all the year
Each vibrant as the Spring.
O what a singing life is there!
No bird is dumb, and all the air
Vibrates with lyric melody
Outpoured in notes of ecstasy
To glory's kingly King.
There Sharon's bright, perennial Rose
In God's immortal garden grows
Distilling fragrance round.

Immanuel's Land! how high, how fair!
And bought at cost beyond compare
In anguish, grief and blood.
No sinner-tongue can ever trace
The shining wonders of that face
That bore in patient majesty
Our bitter curse and penalty –
The stricken Lamb of God.
A vanquished grave is all the price
We pay to enter Paradise,
For Christ has drawn the sting.

Immanuel's Land! how high, how fair!
Full recompense for every tear,
For every wound and scar.
How sweet that first unclouded view
Of Christ, long-loved, yet strangely new:
As new as summer's early rose,
Yet sought long since like night's repose
To pilgrims from afar.

5 'The rose is neighbour to the thorn'.

6 'I can but wait upon the bank until God's wind shall blow'.

Lady Boyd

Then let earth's shadows flee away,
Till morning of that long, long day
Break on our waiting sight!

TO LADY ARDROSS
(On the death of her mother, Lady Boyd)
London, February 1646
Letter 321

A PRAYER FOR REVIVAL

*'O fairest among all the sons of men, O most excellent One, come home
again! come home, and win the praises and blessings of the mourners in
Zion, the prisoners of hope, that wait for Thee! I know that He can also
triumph in suffering, and weep and reign, and die and triumph, . . .
but how happy were I to see the coronation-day of Christ.'*

Come home again!
O fairest of the sons of men,
Most excellent in earth and heaven.
This only would our hearts implore:
Come to our darkened land once more,
Come home and reign.

Come home again,
And win the blessing and the praise
Of those who mourn for Zion's ways –
The prisoners of hope, who wait
Expectant still at heaven's gate,
Till Christ come forth.

Our hearts know well:
That dying He may triumphs gain,
In weakness conquer still and reign,
Imprisoned may subdue His foes,
Or weeping bear His people's woes –
Our suffering King;

Yet sweeter far
To greet His coronation day,
When all His foes shall melt away,
And this sad earth exultant ring
With shouts of joy, for Christ our King
Comes home to reign.

TO LADY BOYD
Aberdeen, 1637
Letter 210

MARION M'NAUGHT

In 1863 a Kirkcudbright gravedigger was at his work when suddenly his spade struck something hard. With a little further investigation a long-lost grave stone, blackened with age, was revealed. This was the stone that marked the spot where Marion M'Naught had been buried over two hundred years earlier. Surprisingly, there is little else available to tell us of the life of this remarkable woman, and yet her name will never be forgotten while the *Letters of Samuel Rutherford* are read and loved by Christian people.

Marion M'Naught was Rutherford's principal correspondent, and some forty-seven of his letters are addressed to her. These in themselves are an adequate memorial, since a careful study of them provides warm and personal details about Marion M'Naught which would otherwise have been forgotten.

She was born in 1585 into an old and honourable Scottish family and was closely related to the House of Kenmure through her mother, Margaret Gordon, who was the sister of Sir John Gordon of Lochinvar, later Lord Kenmure. When we first encounter Marion M'Naught through the pages of Rutherford's letters in 1627, we find her married to William Fullerton, Provost of Kirkcudbright, and the mother of three children. It was in this year that Samuel Rutherford had settled at nearby Anwoth, and there began a life-long friendship and correspondence between him and the Provost of Kirkcudbright together with his capable wife whose maiden name remained best known to posterity.

Even from a cursory reading of these letters it is evident that Marion M'Naught was a woman of uncommon natural abilities. Again and again Rutherford discussed with her the troubling issues that threatened the cause of true religion amongst the Scottish churches, and most particularly the attempts of the monarchy to enforce episcopacy on a church dedicated to the noble and biblical traditions established by John Knox. These matters weighed heavily on the hearts of the Lord's people and many were prepared to suffer and even to die for the principles they held so dear.

Both Marion M'Naught and her husband, who occupied so prominent a position in Kirkcudbright, were called upon to endure a measure of suffering for Christ's sake, and Rutherford

[51]

often wrote words of encouragement to them both to hold fast their testimony in an evil day:

'Be patient, for the Lord's sake, under the wrongs that you suffer of the wicked . . . You may not be above your Master; many a black stroke received innocent Jesus.'

(Letter 14)

It is clear from the correspondence that there existed a warm and godly affinity of heart and thought between Samuel Rutherford and Marion M'Naught. She loved to attend his ministry and we often read of her presence at the Communion seasons in Anwoth. Rutherford, on his part, felt able to confide to her many of the perplexities and cares that troubled him, and earnestly desired her prayers both for himself and for others. Although he frequently discourses on church affairs in his letters to Marion M'Naught, it is to her that he also entrusts some of his most exalted experiences of Christ – experiences strangely rare among us. Writing from his lonely confinement in Aberdeen, Rutherford says:

'I will not smother nor conceal the kindness of my King Jesus. He hath broken in upon the poor prisoner's soul, like the swelling of Jordan. I am bank and brim full; a great, high spring-tide of the consolations of Christ have overflowed me . . . The Bridegroom's love hath run away with my heart. O love, love, love! Oh, sweet are my royal King's chains! I care not for fire nor torture.'

(Letter 279)

Above everything else, Marion M'Naught was a woman of prayer, and in her heart there burned a passionate concern for the welfare of Christ's church and for a revival of true religion in the land. She gave herself to continual prayer and fasting to this end – so much so that Rutherford feared for her health. 'Remember you are in the body, and it is the lodging house;' he warns, 'and you may not, without offending the Lord, suffer the old walls of that house to fall down through want of necessary food' (Letter 26). At times she was sorely discouraged, because it appeared that the earnest prayers she had sent heavenward were of no avail, and Rutherford writes to stimulate and encourage this faithful intercessor: 'I charge you . . . to go on without fainting or fear, and still believe, and take no nay-say. If ye leave off, the field is lost' (Letter 221; see poem, *Unforgotten Prayers*).

In fact, just a year after these words were written, Marion M'Naught saw her longings abundantly fulfilled in the extraordinary scenes of revival that accompanied the signing of the National Covenant in 1638. John Gillies, in his *Historical Collections of Accounts of Revival*[1], quotes Robert Fleming's contemporary account of those days: 'Since the land was engaged by covenant to the Lord . . . what a solemn outletting of the Spirit hath been seen, a large harvest with much of the fruit of the Gospel discernible, which . . . hath been proved in the inbringing of thousands to Christ.'

Marion M'Naught maintained a close contact with her great friend and relative, Lady Kenmure, and when Sir John was dying, he requested the presence of his niece under his roof to attend him through his last illness. She heard, with others, the moving words of Lord Kenmure as he lay on his deathbed, and must have marvelled and grieved, together with his young wife. She would have listened to the dying man ask, 'What is Christ like that I may know Him?' and heard Rutherford's reply, 'He is like love and all lovely' – words entirely characteristic of the whole spirit of this godly man.

If no adequate memorials exist to commemorate the life of Marion M'Naught who died in 1643, none could wish a finer epitaph than words of Samuel Rutherford concerning her:

'Blessed be the Lord! that in God's mercy I found in this country such a woman, to whom Jesus is dearer than her own heart.'

(Letter 22)

[1] First Banner of Truth Trust edition 1981: p.201.

UNFORGOTTEN PRAYERS

*'Faint not, keep breath, believe; howbeit men, and husband, and
friends prove weak, yet your strength faileth not . . . It is your glory to
lay hold on your Rock. O woman greatly beloved! I testify and avouch
it in my Lord, that the prayers ye sent to heaven these many years bygone
are come up before the Lord, and shall not be forgotten . . . The bride
will yet sing, as in the days of her youth.'*

O woman greatly loved,
Your prayers are heard on high;
God reads the language of your tears,
And marks the earnest sigh.
Firm is the Rock to which you cleave,
Faint not, keep breath and still believe.

So shall your bow abide
Unshaken in its strength.
Hold fast in faith, though all prove weak
Or weary grow at length.
The field is lost if you should fail
But well-placed hope must soon prevail.

For prayers that rise to God,
Though many years pass by,
Remembered still, wait near His throne,
Beneath His kindly eye.
The God of glory must fulfill
His faithful promises and will.

And mercy shall come down:
For though the bush may burn,
Yet unconsumed it still remains,
Till Christ in mercy turn,
And by His Spirit's quickening breath
Raise up His bride from dust and death.

And she shall sing once more
As in her youthful days,
High songs of praise to her fair King,
While men in wonder gaze.
Then shall the olive bud again
And all Christ's enemies be slain.

TO MARION M'NAUGHT
Aberdeen, 1637
Letter 221

[54]

JOHN GORDON OF CARDONESS

Old John Gordon, the laird of Cardoness Castle, had sown his wild oats in his youth. Even now when old age had robbed him of his fire and subdued his spirit he could still be very obstinate and a hard master of men.

Cardoness Castle stood at the mouth of the River Fleet on a rocky prominence overlooking all the surrounding area of Anwoth. From this gaunt fortress John Gordon had intimidated his farming tenants, often making extortionate demands of them, in a vain attempt to deal with the crippling debts that lay on his small estate.

When young Samuel Rutherford settled in the parish of Anwoth as its first minister, he was quick to denounce the abuses of Cardoness Castle and fearless in his exposure of the sins of its wily old laird. Yet strange as it may seem, an unlikely friendship sprang up between this tough old man and the small fair-haired pastor. For in spite of his unruly temper and rough ways John Gordon was 'not far from the kingdom'.

When Rutherford was removed from his church and exiled in Aberdeen, his concern for John Gordon weighed heavily on his heart and eight letters reached the Castle from that lonely prison. Each of these is filled with earnest exhortations: 'I always saw nature mighty, lofty, heady, and strong in you,' he writes, and then warns, 'Ye will take . . . a deep cut, and a long lance, to go to the bottom of your wounds in saving humiliation, to make you a won prey for Christ' (Letter 82). Rutherford's stringent warnings of the consequences John Gordon would face for the neglect of his soul were enough to strike fear into the boldest heart; yet his words are shot through with tenderness and love, 'Ye are in my heart in the night-watches . . . O Lord, bear me witness, if my soul thirsteth for anything out of heaven, more than for your salvation' (Letter 166; see poem, *Earnest Entreaties with a Friend*).

Rutherford's letters to Lady Cardoness are in a very different vein for she was a faithful Christian seeking to live out her spiritual pilgrimage in difficult circumstances. Often in her hour of need Christ seemed to hide His face and Rutherford applies himself to her case as a true pastor: 'When Christ hideth Himself, wait on, and make din till He return . . . Yet believe His love in a patient onwaiting and believing in the dark' (Letter 100). He deals with her problem of living with a bad-tempered old man with understanding: 'Bear with him when passion overtaketh him . . . and apply yourself in the fear of God to him' (Letter 100). But even Lady Cardoness is warned against exploiting the tenants and constantly reminded that this world is not the portion of Christ's believing people. 'Let not the world be your portion; . . . set your heart on the inheritance. Go up beforehand, and see your lodging. Look through all your Father's rooms in heaven . . .' (Letter 103; see poem, *Stray Affections*).

There is evidence from Letter 124 to suggest that John Gordon responded to Rutherford's earnest injunctions, bowed his proud head, and entered into the kingdom of God. 'Come in, come in to Christ,' Rutherford had urged, 'I dare avouch that ye shall be dearly welcome to Him' (Letter 82). And John Gordon would have found Christ to be altogether lovely as Rutherford had promised:

'I dare say that angels' pens, angels' tongues, nay, as many worlds of angels as there are drops of water in all the seas, and fountains, and rivers of the earth, cannot paint Him out to you . . . His bare shadow were enough for me; . . . Christ, Christ, nothing but Christ, can cool our love's burning languor'.

(Letter 82)

EARNEST ENTREATIES WITH A FRIEND

'Read over your life, with the light of God's day-light and sun; for
salvation is not casten down at every man's door . . . Now, when ye are
drinking the grounds of your cup . . . and old age, like death's long
shadow, is casting a covering upon your days, it is no time to court this
vain life . . . Come in, come in to Christ . . . I dare avouch that ye
shall be dearly welcome to Him . . . Wo, wo is me! that sin hath made
so many madmen, seeking . . . fire under ice . . . Christ, Christ,
nothing but Christ, can cool our love's burning languor.'

Old age, like death's long shadow, draws apace
To cast a mantle on your ways
Of weakness, pain and fear.
The boasted strength of manhood days,
The passing glory of the petty sphere
Must fade without a trace.
Each hoarded gain, each passionate desire
Can then no longer satisfy,
For life's short dream will blaze and die
Like ashes of a fire.

Read well your book of life, O read it well!
Those faithful lines each deed record
In God's unsullied light.
No page may safely be ignored,
O read it well ere evening turns to night
And death your hopes dispel.
Salvation knocks but seldom at the door,
Then open to this gentle guest,
A lodging grant within your breast
Lest He should knock no more.

Stoop, stoop my friend, in meek humility;
Let lofty nature bow its head,
For low is heaven's gate.
Now to this gilded world be dead,
And come, come in to Christ – the hour is late,
Yet welcomed you shall be.

This sin-crazed world seeks fire beneath cold ice,
But Christ, the Source of love's pure fire,
Alone can meet the heart's desire.
Fair Rose of Paradise.

TO JOHN GORDON OF CARDONESS
Aberdeen, 1637
Letter 82

STRAY AFFECTIONS

*'Faint not; because this . . . world is not a home that laugheth upon
you . . . Set not your heart upon the world since God hath not made it
your portion . . . Learn daily both to possess and miss Christ, in His
secret bridegroom-smiles. He must go and come because His infinite
wisdom thinketh it best for you. We shall be together one day.'*

This careless laughing world is not a home
That throws its smiles on you;
So mount by faith to realms on high
Your Father's house to view,
Go up and see your promised lodging-place,
True portion of the heaven-born child of grace.

And daily learn both to possess and miss
Christ's secret bridegroom-smile,
Whose wisdom sees it best that He
Must go and come awhile,
That He might draw your stray affections home
And ground your faltering love on Christ alone.

[58]

John Gordon of Cardoness

How blest the man whose hope with open face
Looks onward to the day
When Christ shall put desertions, loss
And trials out of play!
Nor earth again the heart from God divide
Or sever Christ the Bridegroom from His bride.

TO LADY CARDONESS
Aberdeen, 1637
Letter 192

WILLIAM GORDON OF EARLSTON

Early in life William Gordon learnt what it meant to suffer for Christ's sake. He was the oldest son of Alexander Gordon of Earlston, a man who had continually borne the spoiling of his goods in days when principled Christian men were harried, fined and persecuted for their allegiance to the cause of Christ. Alexander Gordon, who farmed his family estates not far from Anwoth, was a personal friend of Samuel Rutherford. His Christian character has been described by John Livingstone in these words: 'A man of great spirit, but much subdued by inward exercise. For wisdom, courage and righteousness he might have been a magistrate in any part of the earth.' Such a man became the early target for the venom of church leaders opposed to biblical religion. Writing to him shortly before his own banishment to Aberdeen, Rutherford observes: 'Ye are the first man in Galloway called out and questioned for the name of Jesus', and adds, 'Christ hath said, "Alexander Gordon shall lead the ring in witnessing a good confession", and therefore He hath put the garland of suffering for Himself first upon your head' (Letter 59).

William was a worthy son of such a father and early evidenced a godliness of life that drew from the exiled Rutherford letters of extraordinary depth and spirituality. Only four letters are addressed to him, but each is a masterpiece of interpretation, both of Rutherford's own experiences of God and of the problems that perplexed William Gordon.

How encouraging it must have been to a young believer to know that even the saintly Rutherford felt deeply 'the plague of his own heart'. 'I never took it to be so hard to be dead to my lusts and to this world', Rutherford confesses, yet in the same breath urges young Gordon to 'Be greedy of grace. Study above anything . . . to mortify your lusts' (Letter 99). Rutherford assures the troubled young man that even failure and sin can be turned to advantage. 'All Christ's good bairns go to heaven with a broken brow, and with a crooked leg . . . let young and strong corruptions and His free grace be yoked together.' Then with a touch of humour Rutherford refers to all the spiritual complaints that have filled William Gordon's letter and comments: 'He that can tell his tale, and send such a letter to heaven as he hath sent to Aberdeen . . . will come speed with Christ' (Letter 181).

Samuel Rutherford and William Gordon lived in days when life was very insecure for followers of Christ and it is not surprising that these men looked continually to a better country and learnt to suffer with patience the sorrows and deprivations of their earthly lot. Rutherford's sentiments may sometimes seem a little fatalistic, but seen against the backcloth of persecution, they are in reality a resignation to the will of God, and express an unwavering hope in the glory and joy awaiting believers. He writes to young Gordon, who was one day to pay the price of allegiance to Christ's cause with his blood, in the following words:

'I am persuaded that it is a piece of the chief errand of our life . . . that we might suffer for a time here amongst our enemies; otherwise He might have made heaven to wait on us . . . and have carried us home to our country, without letting us set down our feet in this knotty and thorny life . . . Why then should we not laugh at adversity, and scorn our short-born and soon-dying temptations?'

(Letter 196; see poem, *A Prisoner of Hope*)

The remainder of Gordon's life is soon told. Molested continually by his persecutors, fined unmercifully, the family home plundered and he himself banished from the country, he held firmly to his convictions and triumphed through the grace of God alone. At length in 1679, as he attempted to join the Covenanter forces in their vain fight at Bothwell Bridge, he was met by a victorious party of the King's calvary men. At his refusal to yield to their rough demands of surrender, he was shot where he stood and his body thrown into a ditch. So perished a godly and noble man 'of whom the world was not worthy'.

A PRISONER OF HOPE

'I remain still a prisoner of hope, and do think it service to the Lord to wait on still with submission, till the Lord's morning sky break, and His summer day dawn . . . But seeing a piece of suffering is carved to every one of us, less or more, as infinite Wisdom hath thought good . . . what folly is it, to sit down and weep upon a decree of God, that is both deaf and dumb to our tears . . . It were better to make windows in our prison, and to look out to God and our country, heaven.'

Fair and lasting summer day
Shine from under night's dark sky;
For this prisoner of hope
Waits deliverance from on high.

With submissive heart I take
My appointed suffering here,
Knowing that the all-wise God
Carves to each his needful share.
Pent in this poor house of clay
Patiently would I endure
Until Christ shall break time's chain,
Lead me to a fairer shore.

Vain it is to sit and weep
At a deaf and dumb decree
Made before the stars were born,
Planned immutably for me.
Let me rather windows make
In my prison walls to see
Vistas fair in worlds to come,
Far beyond adversity.

Glory soon shall over-pay
Every light, short-dated cross,
Swallow up in endless joy
All my pain, affliction, loss.
Break, O summer morning, break,
Set Christ's hopeful prisoners free –
Free to breathe the King's pure air,
Loosed from all captivity.

TO WILLIAM GORDON OF EARLSTON
Aberdeen, 1637
Letter 196

LADY CULROSS

The account of the amazing acts of God at the Kirk of Shotts in 1630 is well-known to many Christian people and has long been treasured for its part in the history of God's supernatural interventions. There are few, however, who will have heard the name of Elizabeth Melvill or know of her connection with this out-pouring of God's Spirit.

Elizabeth Melvill was a high-born Scottish lady who used her wealth and influence in the cause of Christ. She was the daughter of Sir James Melvill of Halhill, a godly man, and an accomplished statesman and privy councillor to King James VI; and she was the wife of James Colvill, later Lord Culross.

Although a woman of uncommon natural ability and poetic gift, Lady Culross was noteworthy above all for her godliness. John Livingstone, with whom she maintained a regular correspondence and life-long friendship, described her in this way: 'Of all that ever I saw she was the most unwearied in religious exercises, and the more she attained access to God therein, she hungered the more.'

The Communion season held at Shotts during June 1630 was a time of spiritual blessing which has lived on in the annals of Scottish church history. These services were generally held in the open air over a week-end with thousands present from all the surrounding districts. On this occasion some of the best-known preachers of the day had been invited to be present. The week-end had been remarkable in itself, but by Sunday night it became clear that the people were unwilling to disperse, sensing that the Spirit of God was brooding over the place. Lady Culross and many others spent the night wrestling with God in prayer. We may only guess at the intensity of intercession that must have engaged the hearts of those gathered that night, but we know of a certainty that God mightily answered His people's cries. Through the preaching of young John Livingstone on the Monday of the Communion, a great harvest of souls was gathered to Christ. It is known that his name had been suggested by Lady Culross.

Samuel Rutherford's four letters to Lady Culross written from Aberdeen are marked by great frankness and give us a glimpse into the sufferings he felt because he could no longer preach Christ to his people at Anwoth. 'My ebbings are very low', he complains, and exclaims, 'Oh, cruelty! to put out the poor man's one eye; and this was my joy next to Christ, to preach my Well-Beloved' (Letter 222). At times it seemed that even Christ had hidden His face, making his sufferings still more acute. (See poem, *An Absent Christ.*) Yet even as he grieves over his lot his faith rises up in triumph and he is able to write, 'I see grace groweth best in winter' (Letter 74), and in another letter to observe, 'My Lord hath made my cross as if it were all crystal, so as I can see through it Christ's fair face and heaven; and that God hath honoured a lump of sinful flesh and blood the like of me, to be Christ's honourable lord-prisoner' (Letter 178; see poem, *The Banished Pastor's Consolation*).

Lady Culross was often deeply distressed in her family circumstances for, in spite of her rare godliness, most of her children grew up in unbelief. In heaviness of heart she writes: 'Guiltiness in me and mine is my greatest cross. I would, if it were the Lord's will, choose affliction rather than iniquity.' Rutherford deals sympathetically with her problem: 'As for your son, who is your grief, your Lord waited on you and me, till we were ripe, and brought us in. It is your part to pray and wait upon Him' (Letter 222). We know that at least one of her daughters became a source of spiritual consolation to her mother. Despite the sharp blast of winter, the flower of grace flourished with singular beauty in the life of Lady Culross.

7 Kirkcudbright across the River Dee, home of Marion M'Naught, Rutherford's principal correspondent.

8   The banks of Loch Ken. Kenmure Castle is hidden among trees in the
background.

Lady Culross

AN ABSENT CHRIST

*'He hath fettered me with His love, and run away, and left me a
chained man . . . My ebbings are very low, and the tide is far out when
my Belovèd goeth away . . . but my comfort is to lie and wait on, and to
put my poor soul and my sufferings into Christ's hand.'*

Who can discern Christ's secret ways,
For with love's chain He fettered me
Then ran away and left my soul
To mourn in sweet captivity?
I dare not call my Saviour harsh,
Though He may come and go at will,
Feed me with love, then clear the board
And leave my soul a-hungering still.

My tide is low, my sea far out
When my Belovèd goes away;
Yet still I clamour at His door
Nor give Him rest by night or day.
In Christ's kind hand I place my need
Whose bounty is my sole supply;
For my best riches are those wants
That Christ Himself must satisfy.

TO LADY CULROSS
Aberdeen, 1637
Letter 222

THE BANISHED PASTOR'S CONSOLATION

*'I know not whether joy or heaviness in my soul carrieth it away . . .
my Lord hath made my cross as if it were all crystal, so as I can see
through it Christ's fair face and heaven . . . But my Lord, in His sweet
visits, hath done more . . . for . . . He will be a confined prisoner with
me. He lieth down and riseth up with me; when I sigh, He sigheth;
when I weep, He suffereth with me . . .'*

A borrowed house, a borrowed bed,
A fire, though not my own;
My sorrows these, but greater far
This grief my heart has known:
A scattered flock beyond my reach
And silent lips that long to preach.

Yet Christ has come to share my lot,
With me to lie or stand,
To weep with me, then wipe each tear
With His own kingly hand.
Most sweet the visits He bestows,
Till beautiful my prison grows.

This cross though weighty still and hard
Is made of crystal clear,
And through its pure transparency
I see Christ's face so fair.
No longer cheerless is my cell,
When He is pleased with me to dwell.

My heaviness is mixed with joy,
For love has cast my chain;
His consolations swallow up
My tale of short-lived pain.
Then let my sufferings preach his name
A silenced tongue His love proclaim!

TO LADY CULROSS
June 1637
Letter 178

[66]

LADY ROBERTLAND

Lady Robertland of Stewarton was described by Robert Blair, a contemporary preacher, as 'that famous saint' and although few details of her life are known, she was clearly much used by God to her generation.

During the years 1625–1630 a powerful revival had swept through the West of Scotland affecting all the area around Stewarton. Robert Fleming's account of those days demonstrates the profound effect this outpouring of God's Spirit had upon the people: 'Many were so choked and taken by the heart . . . in hearing of the word they have been made to fall over and thus carried out of the church; who afterwards proved most solid and useful Christians.' Some mockingly called these strong convictions of sin 'the Stewarton sickness' but it was during this very period that Lady Robertland was most greatly used of God. Her home became a refuge for many who had been awakened under the preaching of the gospel.

God had evidently been preparing Lady Robertland for this service, for John Livingstone tells us that she was 'one deeply exercised in her mind' and one who 'often got rare outgates'. By this quaint expression he means that she had known many remarkable deliverances from God in times of distress. Through these experiences God had well-fitted Lady Robertland to help those in spiritual need.

Livingstone also tells us that Lady Robertland had an unusual gift for seeing spiritual parallels and parables in all the normal events of her life, and of continually using these figures of speech in her conversations. It is not surprising therefore that when Samuel Rutherford writes to Lady Robertland he takes up her own strange mode of expression and in almost every sentence uses symbolic language and unusual imagery. So to one who had known so many 'rare outgates', he writes:

'If He would come in, I shall not dispute the matter, where He get a hole, or how He opened the lock . . . He hath a gate of His own beyond the thoughts of men, that no foot hath skill to follow Him . . .'.

(Letter 282; see poem, *Christ's Secret Gate*)

[67]

CHRIST'S SECRET GATE

'I see there is a sort of impatient patience required in the want of Christ as to His manifestations, and waiting on. They thrive who wait on His love . . . and . . . in that on-waiting, make haste and din and much ado for their lost and hidden Lord Jesus . . . He hath a gate of His own beyond the thoughts of men, that no foot hath skill to follow Him.'

Christ has a gate far beyond all our thinking –
Hidden the key, and the lock no man knows;
Free as the wind in His secret appearings,
Sweetly He comes and then strangely He goes.

Ours but to seek Him with impatient patience!
They only thrive who will wait for His love,
Yet in the waiting besiege Him with weeping,
Making ado till He come from above.

Christ by His dealings would fashion and mould us;
Carving out baseness, corruption and sin,
Making us perfect by pain and by wounding,
Forming His Father's fair image within.

Daily we mar all our prospects of heaven,
Stumbling we falter, yet Christ makes us whole;
Kindly He lifts us with glimpses of glory,
Till all its splendour shall rise on our soul.

TO LADY ROBERTLAND
Aberdeen, January 1638
Letter 282

JOHN KENNEDY OF AYR

Old Hugh Kennedy, the Provost of Ayr, was a spiritual giant even in an age of great men. He was a friend and contemporary of John Welsh the godly minister of Ayr who wrote of him, 'Happy is that city, yea happy is that nation that has a Hugh Kennedy in it'. Two outstanding features of this man's life have come down to us through the years. The first was the way he prayed. He is described as 'a mighty wrestler with God', and on one occasion the progress of the plague in the town of Ayr is said to have been halted in answer to his petitions. The second was the way he died. We are told by Wodrow in his life of *Boyd of Trochrig* that on his death-bed Kennedy 'was filled with inexpressible joy in the Holy Ghost beyond what it is possible to comprehend'.

His son, John Kennedy, was also a man of fine Christian character. We read of him that 'he was as choice a Christian as any at that time'. The high spiritual tone of the three letters that Rutherford wrote to him bear out this testimony.

On one occasion John Kennedy experienced a remarkable deliverance from death in a storm. John Stuart, a close friend of his and also one of Rutherford's correspondents, had been plunged into financial straits after receiving news that a ship he owned, laden with goods, had been captured by the Turks. In the event this report proved false, and great was the jubilation among the men of Ayr when the missing vessel appeared on the horizon. In much excitement John Kennedy put out to sea in a small boat to greet the ship's return. But joy soon turned to horror as a fierce storm sprang up. To the anxious men on the shore it appeared that the little boat had been swallowed up by the waves. Even the large vessel seemed to be in imminent danger. Heart-broken Stewart returned home and shut himself up in his room to mourn a loss far more grievous than that of his vessel.

After three days Stewart came out of his seclusion and went to visit Kennedy's bereaved wife. It is not hard to imagine his astonishment and delight when at that very moment John Kennedy himself walked in at the door. His boat had been driven from sight beyond the large vessel and eventually grounded on some distant part of the coast.

Samuel Rutherford was quick to take advantage of this amazing providence of God and used it to urge his friend to be well-prepared for death whenever it should strike. Although John Kennedy had witnessed the glorious departure of his father, Rutherford knew that it takes more than example to cause a man to die well. So he writes:

'The last tide will not wait you for one moment. If ye forget anything, when your sea is full, and your foot in that ship, there is no returning again to fetch it . . . ye can die but once, and if ye mar or spill that business, ye cannot come back to mend that piece of work again . . . The number of your months is written in God's book; . . . Fulfil your course with joy, for we take nothing to the grave with us, but a good or evil conscience.'

(Letter 22; see poem, Die Well)

John Kennedy of Ayr

DIE WELL

*'Ye were knocking at these [i.e. death's] black gates, and ye found the
doors shut . . . I trust that ye know that it is not for nothing that ye are
sent to us again. The Lord knew . . . that your armour was not as yet
thick enough against the stroke of death. Now, in the strength of
Jesus . . . end your journey ere the night come upon you. Have all in
readiness against the time that ye must sail through that black and
impetuous Jordan; and Jesus, Jesus, who knoweth both those depths
and the rocks, and all the coasts, be your pilot.'*

But entry was denied – the door was locked;
For Christ who holds the key of death
Bade you return, restored your breath,
Your life He kindly spared.
For He who reads the heart, knew well
The armour of your soul was unprepared
To foil the Prince of hell.

Now in the strength of Jesus rise with haste,
Your eager course fulfil with joy, nor waste
The lingering hours of time's short day;
For evening falls and beckons you away
To stand before the gate.
And then, die well, for life's last tide
Must swiftly ebb and will for no man wait
One moment more beside.

Die well, and Christ the Master of the grave
Will pilot you through death's impetuous wave;
He knows the rocks, the shifting sand,
The proud winds bow before His least command.
It is but once we die,
And none returns to try again;
Then well prepare, till you with joy reply,
'For me to die is gain'.

TO JOHN KENNEDY
*(after deliverance from almost
certain death in a storm)
Anwoth, February 1632
Letter 22*

GEORGE GILLESPIE

George Gillespie lay dying. Although only in his thirties he had already distinguished himself as one of the most outstanding theologians of his generation. Writing to him on his deathbed Samuel Rutherford was able to say: 'Christ in and by you hath done more than by twenty, yea, an hundred grey-haired and godly pastors', and with his death Scotland was to lose one of her ablest defenders of the faith.

In 1634 young Gillespie, son of John Gillespie, minister of the Gospel in Kirkcaldy, became chaplain to Lord and Lady Kenmure. It was here that he first met the pastor of nearby Anwoth and, though Gillespie was but 21 years of age, a warm friendship sprang up between the two men. Both lived in turbulent times for the church of Jesus Christ and both faced a hazardous future. Threats of persecution and banishment hovered over many who were not prepared to bow to the pressure of the State to compromise their faith. So it is not hard to imagine them walking together along the banks of the beautiful Loch Ken, deep in conversation, or kneeling to pray together among the woods that surrounded Kenmure Castle.

Soon Gillespie was to leave the Castle to take up the ministry in Wemyss, but before separating he and Rutherford bound themselves to each other in a solemn covenant of love and friendship. Like David and Jonathan they swore each to remain faithful to the other, to pray for one another and to share the dealings of God with their souls.

Only three letters have been preserved to us of the many that must have passed between them. In two of these Rutherford, banished to Aberdeen far from his beloved Anwoth, reminds Gillespie of their covenant and earnestly solicits his prayers: 'Brother, remember our old covenant, pray for me and write to me your case', he urges.

They were reunited in London in 1643 when for four long years they laboured alongside the finest of the English theologians on the task of drawing up the great Westminster Confession of Faith. It was in this context that Gillespie's most brilliant gifts as a shrewd and eloquent debater and a discerning theologian became apparent. Robert Baillie, another of the four Commissioners chosen to represent the Scottish Church, could look round the entire gathering of learned and godly men and declare: 'I admire the gifts of that noble youth Mr Gillespie and bless God for him in particular as equal to the first in the Assembly.'

Scarcely a year after the completion of the Confession, Gillespie was dying. Although he faced death without fear, Gillespie knew very little of the comforting sense of the presence of Christ as he lay on his deathbed. Sometimes his sins and shortcomings rose up in frightening array before his eyes, and then the eternal city seemed hidden from view and his mind became distressed with dark and troubling thoughts.

It was at such a time that Rutherford proved a friend indeed both by his letters and by his visits to Kirkcaldy where Gillespie lay. He urged his friend to look away from his failures and to rest only in Christ's righteousness. 'If ye look to yourself as divided from Christ, ye must be more than heavy. All your wants, dear brother, be upon Him.' Although heaven might seem unreal and doubts and anxieties undermine his spiritual confidence, Rutherford constantly directed his friend to look beyond his present distress to the certain joys that awaited him. 'Look to the east', he wrote, 'the dawning of the glory is near . . . It is all keeping that ye would now have, till ye need it' (Letter 324; see poem, *To a Dying Friend*).

Such words of consolation must surely have encouraged the dying man to utter his simple yet moving reply: 'Though the Lord allow me no comfort yet I will *believe* that my Belovèd is mine and I am His.' And so, protesting that it was 'reward enough that ever I got leave to do Christ any service', this Valiant-for-Truth passed through the last river in triumph. His loss was deeply felt by all the Scottish Church and by his family, while Rutherford could write sadly, 'I dare say nothing against His dispensation. I hope to follow quickly' (Letter 324).

George Gillespie

TO A DYING FRIEND

*'I cannot speak to you. The way ye know; . . . the print of the footsteps
of the Forerunner is clear and manifest; many have gone before
you . . . Look to the east, the dawning of the glory is near. Your Guide
is good company, and knoweth all the miles, and the ups and downs in
the way . . . Some travellers see the city . . . at a distance; and yet
within the eighth part of a mile they cannot see it . . .'*

Mute I must stand and watch you die
For words seem all in vain,
Nor dare I let my murmuring lips
Against my God complain.

The way you know for Christ has walked
The untried path before;
Indelible His heavenward print
On time's elusive shore.
This self-same track the saints of old
In ages past have trod;
And you with all Christ's younger heirs
Press homeward to your God.

The night, you say, is dark and long,
The city out of sight;
Yet lift your eyes: look to the east
Where shadows take their flight.
And though the goal seem wreathed in mists
Still cleave to Christ your Guide
Whose hidden love reserves for you
Those comforts now denied.

But one fight more – one fight of faith –
The bravest and the last;
One act of firm believing then
The conflict shall be past.
On Christ's strong righteousness rely
Nor gaze on all your sin;
Grace signs each debt as fully paid,
Declares the guilty clean.

To Him commit your deathless soul,
Your weakness to His strength,
Until your faltering steps shall gain
Immanuel's land at length.

TO GEORGE GILLESPIE
St Andrews, September 1648
Letter 324

ROBERT GORDON OF KNOCKBREX

Robert Gordon's family home was delightfully situated among the thick woods that sloped down towards Wigtown Bay in Galloway. The old home has long been demolished and replaced, but the woods and sands of Knockbrex could bear testimony to the memory of Robert Gordon.

In one of his terse word-pictures of Christian men and women known to him, John Livingstone describes Robert Gordon as 'a single-hearted and painful Christian,' and it is not surprising that the pastor of nearby Anwoth should soon find companionship and consolation in the company of such a man.

Robert Gordon's unwavering affections were evident in the concern he showed for the cause of Christ. In the correspondence that passed between Rutherford and Gordon they often shared their mutual longings that God would again look with favour upon His church in Scotland. We are not surprised to find that this single-hearted man was present at the signing of the National Covenant in 1638 – a document that many were prepared to sign with pens dipped in blood. Often Gordon's dedication to the interests of Christ's Kingdom meant long periods away from the secluded comforts of home, for after 1638 he spent much of his time in public meetings and parliamentary business.

It is not so clear what Livingstone meant when he described Robert Gordon as 'a painful Christian,' but the term suggests that he was a man who was painstaking in his determination to grow in grace and to root out the sins still latent within him. It also infers that his conscience was deeply sensitive: so sensitive perhaps that he often fell into despair about his own spiritual condition. Whether or not that is so, it is to this 'painful Christian' that Rutherford writes some of the best-known and best-loved words to be found anywhere in his three hundred and sixty-five letters:

'Oh, what owe I to the file, to the hammer, to the furnace of my Lord Jesus! who hath now let me see how good the wheat of Christ is, that goeth through His mill . . . to be made bread for His own table. Grace tried is better than grace, and it is more than grace; it is glory in its infancy . . . Why should I start at the plough of my Lord, that maketh deep furrows on my soul? I know that He is no idle Husbandman, He purposeth a crop.'

(Letter 76; see poem, *The Trial of Grace*).

[77]

THE TRIAL OF GRACE

*'Grace tried is better than grace, and it is more than grace; it is glory in
its infancy . . . Why should I start at the plough of my Lord, that
maketh deep furrows on my soul? I know that He is no idle
Husbandman, He purposeth a crop.'*

Why should I fear if on my soul
My Master's plough draws furrows deep?
No idle Husbandman is He
Who purposes a crop to reap.
This fallow ground He ploughs with pain,
A harvest full at length to gain.

Grace tried is more than grace and grows
To glory in its infancy!
And who can tell the truth of grace
Till trial prove its constancy?
Today the hammer, file and heat,
The next His handiwork complete.

So let each cross breathe out His love,
Each tell His wisdom, kindness, care;
Each speak with unloosed tongue His worth
Who crowns my head with garlands fair.
This prison is my house of wine,
Here Christ and I may richly dine.

TO ROBERT GORDON OF KNOCKBREX
Aberdeen, 1637
Letter 76

ALEXANDER GORDON OF KNOCKGRAY

Alexander Gordon of Knockgray was 'a rare Christian in his time' as John Livingstone quaintly tells us in his brief pen-portrait. The old Knockgray homestead nestled at the foot of the hills of Carsphairn in Galloway and here Alexander Gordon passed his quiet days farming his vast flocks of sheep that numbered over ten thousand animals.

Life had not always been this way: for Alexander Gordon was another Christian man who had been prepared to suffer in days when true religion was under threat from those wishing to enforce pre-Reformation forms on the Scottish churches. Lord Kenmure's father had expelled Gordon from home and lands because of his uncompromised Christian principles, and he had been imprisoned in Edinburgh for some time. When Lord Kenmure inherited his father's title and position he restored the good man to his possessions. Like Job of old it could be said of Alexander Gordon that the Lord blessed his latter end more than the beginning, and Gordon himself was the first to ascribe his prosperity to the goodness of God.

It would appear that he was elderly by the time Rutherford became acquainted with him. Writing to Gordon from Aberdeen Rutherford says, 'Christ's ways were known to you long before I, who am but a child, knew anything of Him'. With the appointment of Thomas Sydserff as prelate – the very man who had relentlessly hounded Rutherford out of Anwoth – persecution again seemed to threaten the men of Galloway. Rutherford urges:

'Contend to the last breath for Christ . . . Fear nothing; for I assure you that Alexander Gordon of Knockgray shall win away . . . And what can he then want that is worth the having?'

(Letter 154)

Rutherford had long regarded himself as one of 'God's spies' sent to spy out the land of persecution and imprisonment and to bring back a report of Christ's goodness and support in such circumstances. In this way he sought to encourage all who might be called to tread the same path. There is hardly a more triumphant letter in the whole collection than the one to Alexander Gordon containing these words:

'My prison is my palace, my sorrow is with child of joy, my losses are

[79]

rich losses, my pain easy pain, my heavy days are holy and happy days . . . Oh, if I could set all tongues . . . to work, to help me to sing a new song of my Well-belovèd!'

(Letter 182; see poem, *When Christ Comes*)

Alexander Gordon of Knockgray

WHEN CHRIST COMES

'A cross for Christ should have another name; yea, a cross, especially when He cometh with His arms full of joys, is the happiest hard tree that ever was laid up on my weak shoulder.'

A cross with Christ's own presence blest
Deserves another name,
For when He comes – arms full of joy –
He sets the heart aflame.
No harder, happier tree was yet
On my weak shoulder laid
For Christ and His fair cross to me
Sweet company are made.

This sorrow bears a child of joy,
My pain is easy pain,
My prison to a palace turns
My loss to richest gain.
For Christ has come and on my head
Poured out His spikenard rare,
And hard it is to smother love
Or hide its fragrance fair.

Then let me sing a song of love
Till every tongue unite
To sound my well-Belovèd's worth
And tune His praise aright.

TO ALEXANDER GORDON OF KNOCKGRAY
1637
Letter 182

JOHN GORDON AT RUSCO

On a wooded slope about two miles from Anwoth, Rusco Castle stands in lonely state, telling its silent story of days long past. The castle belonged to Lord and Lady Kenmure and here they lived for a short period during the early days of Rutherford's ministry at Anwoth.

In 1637 another John Gordon and his family – yet one more of the numerous Gordon clan who figure in the pages of Samuel Rutherford's letters – lived at Rusco Castle. During Rutherford's exile in Aberdeen the spiritual condition of many of his parishioners caused him constant concern. 'I have heard,' he writes, 'and my soul is grieved for it, that since my departure from you, many among you are turned back from the good old way' (Letter 225). It is evident from the three letters sent to John Gordon that this man fell into that category and each of these letters follows a similar theme: the emptiness of this world, the brevity of life and the importance of living in a way that gives evidence of true repentance and faith.

Some of the warnings are very stringent, designed to make this worldly nobleman tremble and take stock of his life before it is too late. 'Misspend not your short sand-glass, which runneth very fast; seek your Lord in time', Rutherford urges. He intimates that death will soon overtake him, and then 'This clay-idol, the world, would seem to you . . . not worth a fig; time will eat you out of possession of it. When . . . the imprisoned soul looketh out of the windows of the clay house, ready to leap out into eternity, what would you then give for a lamp full of oil? Oh seek it now' (Letter 147).

Warm exhortations go side by side with the warnings and mark Rutherford out as a true pastor of men. 'Let your heart be set upon finishing of your journey . . . Oh how blessed shall ye be to have a joyful welcome of your Lord at night' (Letter 280; see poem, *This Vain World*).

We do not know whether John Gordon heeded Rutherford's words, but the final letter the exiled pastor wrote describes how far it is possible to go in the path of religion and yet fall short of eternal life at the last. This letter has brought many another reader to a solemn consideration of these issues:

'Remember, many go far on and reform many things, and can find tears, as Esau did; and suffer hunger for truth, as Judas did . . . and profess fair, and fight for the Lord, as Saul did . . . and hear the word of God gladly, and reform their life in many things according to the word, as Herod did; and say to Christ, "Master, I will follow Thee whithersoever Thou goest", as the man who offered to be Christ's servant . . . And yet all these are but like gold in clink and colour, and watered brass, and base metal.'

(Letter 280)

THIS VAIN WORLD

'I find this world, when I have looked upon it on both sides, within and without, and when I have seen even the laughing and lovely side of it, to be but a fool's idol, a clay prison . . . I recommend Christ and His love to you, let Him have the flower of your heart . . . Set a low price on all things but Christ . . . Your forenoon is already spent . . . Let your heart be set on finishing of your journey.'

I have looked on this vain world:
Looked on it without, within,
Seen its laughing, lovely side,
Heard its tale of tears and sin.
As a little child may grasp
Shadows in his outstretched arms,
Find them but a fantasy,
Empty and elusive charms,
So time's children blindly chase
Golden dreams and gods of clay;
Gather for their happiness
Flowers that wither in a day.

Life's short hand-breath soon will pass,
Restless time must take its flight,
Morning wear to afternoon,
Evening fade to shades of night.
Then the poor imprisoned soul
Whimpering in its house of clay
Finds its lovers broken reeds,
Helpless in an evil day.

Set up Christ in all your thought,
Price down every good beside;
Never can your idol-sins
God's great summons-day abide.
Let your hope with one long leap
Bound across life's plastered fun,
Sin's deceitful, foil-wrapped treats,
Rest on heaven's love-worthy One.

John Gordon at Rusco

Make of Him your heart's fair flower,
Christ the yolk of your delight;
Till He greet your journey's end
With a welcome home at night.

TO JOHN GORDON AT RUSCO
Aberdeen, 1637
Letters 147, 272, 280

OTHER CORRESPONDENTS

Over one hundred and fifty people shared the honour of receiving letters from Samuel Rutherford. These were men and women from all strata of society and walks of life. Many were among the nobility of the land and names such as Lady Kenmure, Lady Boyd, Lord Craighall and others figure continually in the letters. Rutherford was equally concerned with those who were of little account in the eyes of men, and when banished to Aberdeen expresses his solicitude for all members of his Anwoth flock. 'Oh if I might but speak to three or four herdboys of my royal Master I would be satisfied' (Letter 163), he declares. We find letters in this collection addressed to those about whom little or nothing is known. The identity of some to whom he writes has been entirely lost or the letter is merely designated 'To a young man in Anwoth'.

A quick glance at the index to *Rutherford's Letters* will give some idea of the breadth of his correspondence. Many ministers of the day are included among these names, but also young Christians whose spiritual needs often drew from Rutherford's pen letters of counsel, encouragement and guidance. Marion M'Naught's daughter, Grizzel, is one to whom he writes in this way, and so also is Lady Boyd's son, Robert.

It is perhaps true to say that Rutherford excels most when he writes to the bereaved. He himself had suffered the loss of his first wife, and eight out of his nine children died in early years. Taught of God in the school of sorrow he was well able to console the broken-hearted. To one who had just lost her husband Rutherford writes:

'In that our Lord took your husband to Himself, I know it was that He might make room for Himself. He cutteth off your love to the creature, that ye might learn that God only is the right owner of your love. Sorrow, loss, sadness, death, are the worst of things that are, except sin. But Christ knoweth well what to make of them . . .'.

(Letter 122; see poem, *Christ's Rough Serjeants*)

If it were possible to assess the spiritual qualities of Rutherford's correspondents by the type of letter that he writes to each, then Jean Brown would shine above many. Only three letters are addressed to this lady, who, we gather, from references elsewhere, was obviously a friend of Marion M'Naught. But each letter is rich in spiritual wisdom and written to one capable of appreciating 'the deep things of God'. She was the mother of John Brown of Wamphray, an able expositor and pastor, who later suffered ejection from his church and banishment for his principles. It is almost as if Rutherford is forewarning Jean Brown of the sufferings which she and her family must endure for Christ's sake, for each of the three letters takes up the theme of the transient nature of this life in comparison with the glory that awaits Christ's believing people. '. . . let your thoughts dwell much upon that blessedness that abideth you in the other world', he says (Letter 111); and again, 'Our sand-glass is not so long as we need to weary; time will eat away and root out our woes and sorrow. Our heaven is in the bud, and growing up to an harvest' (Letter 131; see poem, *Through Brier and Bush*).

Sibylla Macadam is another correspondent about whom little is known; she may have been a relative of Lady Cardoness, and Macadam the eighteenth-century road builder was descended from this family. Only one short letter is addressed to this lady from Aberdeen, but it is a letter of exceptional beauty. It seems to mark a transitional stage of Rutherford's spiritual experience in his bleak northern exile. Gone is the turbulence and distress of mind that characterized the early months of his banishment, and in its place has come a calm born of resignation to the will of God. 'I know that He must be sweet Himself, when His cross is so sweet', he confides; and expresses his submission to God's purposes in these words: 'There is no great reckoning to be made of the withering of my flower, in comparison of the foul and manifest wrongs done to Christ . . . let the bloom fall from my joy, and let it wither, let the Almighty blow out my candle, so being the Lord might be great . . . and His oppressed church delivered' (Letter 193; see poem, *For Me to Live is Christ*).

Samuel Rutherford's Aberdeen experiences confirmed him in the view that 'grace groweth best in Winter'. The testimony that 'God's spy' sent back from the land of exile and suffering can be summed up in words written to John Fullerton of Carleton:

'. . . the greatest temptation out of hell is to live without temptations . . . Faith is the better of the free air, and of the sharp winter storm in its face. Grace withereth without adversity.'
(Letter 157; see poem, *The Greatest Temptation*)

[87]

CHRIST'S ROUGH SERJEANTS

*'You must learn to make your evils your great good; and to spin
comforts . . . out of your troubles, which are Christ's wooers, sent to
speak for you to Himself. It is easy to get good words, and a comfortable
message from our Lord, even from such rough serjeants . . .'*

Sorrow, sickness, death and grieving,
Christ's rough serjeants these,
Sent to draw our wayward footsteps
From a path of ease.

Sent to bring Christ's faithful message,
Kindly words and true,
And from this vain world in pity,
Truant hearts to woo.

Love beneath a veil and hidden
Speaks affection still,
It is enough, let our Beloved
Come which way He will.

Turn then every grief to profit,
Comforts spin from pain,
So may sorrow's consolation,
Work eternal gain.

Hasten, stay not, time's brief evening
Gathers in the west,
And the farther end of sadness
Points our home of rest.

TO A GENTLEWOMAN AFTER THE DEATH
OF HER HUSBAND
Aberdeen
Letter 122

THROUGH BRIER AND BUSH

'*We . . . must set our face against what may befall us in following on,
till He and we be through the briers and bushes, on the dry ground. Our
soft nature would be borne through the troubles of this miserable life in
Christ's arms; and it is His wisdom, who knoweth our mould, that His
bairns go wet-shod and cold-footed to heaven . . . time will eat away
and root out our woes and sorrow. Our heaven is in the bud, and
growing up to an harvest.*'

> Soft nature seeks a path of ease
> Secure from strange alarms;
> Borne through the troubled scenes of life
> In Christ's protecting arms;
> Yet nobler far our strength to draw
> From grace to call His will our law.
>
> For Christ who knows our feeble mould
> Ordains that here below
> Through brier and bush to heavenly ground
> His bairns wet-shod must go;
> Past hostile thorn His steps to trace
> And follow still with steadfast face.
>
> Our heav'n is in the bud and soon
> Must to a harvest grow;
> For time's brief span shall eat away
> And root out every woe.
> Then watch in hope till sorrows end,
> And Christ appear – our living Friend.

TO JEAN BROWN
Aberdeen, March 1637
Letter 131

FOR ME TO LIVE IS CHRIST

'There is no great reckoning to be made of the withering of my flower, in comparison of the foul and manifest wrongs done to Christ. Nay, let never the dew of God lie up on my branches again, let the bloom fall from my joy . . . so being the Lord might be great . . . and His oppressed Church delivered . . . Our joys, besides God, in the inner half are but woes and sorrows. Christ, Christ is that which our love and desires can . . . rest safely upon.'

In bonds am I for Christ my Lord,
Yet all I suffer here
Can never match the grief He knew,
Or with His shame and wrongs compare.
While Christ fares well, what matters it
That I on ashes feed?
And if His weeping Church rejoice,
My burdened heart shall laugh indeed.

What if the dews of God no more
On my poor branches lie,
Or if my fairest bloom should fall,
Or life's brief candle flame and die?
Yet this I know: that Christ is good,
His cross speaks gain untold;
My prison walls are marble-built,
My captive-chain is all of gold.

For heav'n is cast of nobler mould
Than earth's poor clay and mire;
While Christ is mine, I mount with joy
And to the heights of God aspire.
All joys beside are touched with pain,
Worm-eaten is earth's best;
On Christ alone – pure source of love,
Each earthly love can safely rest.

TO SIBYLLA MACADAM
Aberdeen, 1637
Letter 193

[90]

THE GREATEST TEMPTATION

'The greatest temptation out of hell is to live without temptations. If my waters should stand, they would rot. Faith is the better of the free air, and of the sharp winter storm in its face. Grace withereth without adversity. The devil is but God's master fencer, to teach us to handle our weapons.'

Faith fares the best in the sharpness of winter,
Bitter and fierce though the gale in its face;
Strengthened by standing unbowed in the tempest,
Faith may exult in its stormy embrace.

Grace would soon wither and die without conflict,
Striving we conquer in life's battlefield;
Who then is Satan but God's master fencer
Teaching us well every weapon to wield?

Great the temptation to face no temptations;
Long-standing waters may soon stagnant grow;
Seeds sown in weeping midst nature's corruption,
Bring forth a harvest of glory below.

TO JOHN FULLERTON OF CARLETON
Aberdeen, March 1637
Letter 157

SOME OTHER BANNER OF TRUTH TITLES

LETTERS OF SAMUEL RUTHERFORD

Selected by ANDREW A. BONAR

'What a wealth of spiritual ravishment we have here! Rutherford is beyond all praise of men. Like a strong-winged eagle he soars into the highest heaven and with unblenched eye he looks into the mystery of love divine. There is, to us, something mysterious, awe-creating and superhuman about Rutherford's letters.

'This edition is a noble volume, and we shall measure the soundness of Scotch religion very much by the sale of this work. One page of Rutherford is worth a thousand tomes of the Downgrade frothiness.

'We think it meet to take a paragraph from Dr Andrew Bonar's prefatory sketch:

The extravagence in sentiment alleged against them by some is just that of Paul, when he spoke of knowing 'the height and depth, length and breadth' of the love of Christ; or that of Solomon when the Holy Ghost inspired him to write 'The Song of Songs'. Rather would we say of these letters what John Livingstone, in a letter, says of John Welsh's dying words: 'O for a sweet fill of this fanatic humour!' In modern days Richard Cecil has said of Rutherford, 'He is one of my classics; he is a real original'; and in older times, Richard Baxter, some of whose theological leanings might have prejudiced him, if anything could, said of his Letters, 'Hold off the Bible, such a book the world never saw'.

'When we are dead and gone let the world know that Spurgeon held Rutherford's Letters to be the nearest thing to inspiration which can be found in all the writings of mere men'.

C. H. Spurgeon in *The Sword and Trowel, 1891*

768 pp. Cloth-bound

MEMOIR AND REMAINS OF ROBERT MURRAY M'CHEYNE

ANDREW A. BONAR

Few books have been better loved than the *Memoir and Remains of R. M. M'Cheyne*. Its circulation underlines this. First published in 1844, within twenty-five years it went through one hundred and sixteen editions. In 1910 it was estimated that including translations into other languages not less than half a million copies were in circulation.

Few books have had such a widespread influence on the lives of God's people. Testimonies to its usefulness were received from many lands and Christians of differing theological persuasions have testified to the blessing experienced through reading it. 'This is one of the best and most profitable volumes ever published', said C. H. Spurgeon. 'The memoir of such a man ought surely to be in the hands of every Christian, and certainly every preacher of the Gospel.'

Few books contain such variety and wealth of spiritual matter between their covers. As well as the life, covering 174 pages, the work contains a good selection of letters (126 pages), sermons (203 pages), other writings (86 pages) and sacred songs (18 pages).

664 pp. Cloth-bound

MEMOIRS OF THOMAS BOSTON

Born into relative obscurity in 1676 in Duns, Berwickshire, Thomas Boston died in 1732 in the small parish of Ettrick in the Scottish Borders. But his 56 year life, 45 of them spent in conscious Christian discipleship, lend credibility to the spiritual principle that it is not *where* a Christian serves, but *what quality* of service he renders, that really counts.

While Jonathan Edwards wrote that he was 'a truly great divine', it is as a loving, faithful, rigorously self-disciplined Christian pastor that Boston is best remembered. Leaving his first charge at Simprin (where he served 1699–1707), he settled in Ettrick for a 25-year ministry. Constantly burdened for his congregation, Boston taught them in season and out of season, in pulpit and in home; burdened for the truth of the gospel, he overcame all natural timidity to engage in controversy over the teaching of Professor Simson (who was charged with heretical doctrine), and in the famous 'Marrow Controversy'.

It is, however, as a preacher that Boston's influence was most widely felt; 'There was a grip in it that no preacher wins who is a stranger to his own heart'. Out of this ministry came *Human Nature in Its Fourfold State* and other works of enduring value.

Boston's *Memoirs* record the joys and sorrows, the burdens and victories of his life. Here we read of his love for Catherine Brown and of their marriage, of death in the family circle, of the dark cloud of his wife's affliction, and of Boston's own ceaseless gospel labours. Out of these labours, and his deep Christian experience, Thomas Boston gave the church one of its most enduring spiritual autobiographies.

576pp. Cloth-bound

For complete catalogue, listing over 300 titles, write to:

THE BANNER OF TRUTH TRUST
3 Murrayfield Road, Edinburgh EH12 6EL
P O Box 621, Carlisle, Pennsylvania 17013, USA